SpringerBriefs in Law

SpringerBriefs present concise summaries of cutting-edge research and practical applications across a wide spectrum of fields. Featuring compact volumes of 50 to 125 pages, the series covers a range of content from professional to academic. Typical topics might include:

- A timely report of state-of-the art analytical techniques
- A bridge between new research results, as published in journal articles, and a contextual literature review
- A snapshot of a hot or emerging topic
- A presentation of core concepts that students must understand in order to make independent contributions

SpringerBriefs in Law showcase emerging theory, empirical research, and practical application in Law from a global author community. SpringerBriefs are characterized by fast, global electronic dissemination, standard publishing contracts, standardized manuscript preparation and formatting guidelines, and expedited production schedules

More information about this series at http://www.springer.com/series/10164

Ali Shirvani

Transnational Evaluation of Constitutions

Through the Prism of Human Rights and International Law

Springer

Ali Shirvani
School of Oriental and African Studies
Xi'an International Studies University
Xi'an, China

Center for China and Globalization
Beijing, China

ISSN 2192-855X ISSN 2192-8568 (electronic)
SpringerBriefs in Law
ISBN 978-981-16-2975-4 ISBN 978-981-16-2976-1 (eBook)
https://doi.org/10.1007/978-981-16-2976-1

This Springer imprint is published by the registered company Springer Nature Singapore Pte Ltd.
The registered company address is: 152 Beach Road, #21-01/04 Gateway East, Singapore 189721, Singapore

"This important study uses novel quantitative and qualitative methods to explore the relationship between constitutional and international law. It is a significant contribution to the literature, and pushes us further toward rigorous analysis of transnational legal regimes."

—Tom Ginsburg, *Professor of Political Science, Chicago Law School*

Dedicated to We the People of the International Community

Preface

After the rise of Arab Spring and violations of the people rights in the forgoing revolutions and later the engagement of the United Nations and international law subjects, both in pre-revolution and later in the establishment, processes of the interim councils for constitutional matters, the idea that was such a violation of rights and threats to the peace preventable from international law point, was in my mind.

The idea turned to a proposal first as a project under discussion to become a Max Planck Institute for Comparative Public Law and International Law when accepted as a Ph.D. proposal in the Law School of Xiamen University 2013.

The questions about this proposal's main idea were how to connect international law and national law with the challenge that international relations and constitutional matters are separated from sovereignty borders, i.e., the challenge was how to connect studies of constitutions as national matters to international law?

The sample of the Libya Revolt of 2011, where the United Nations Security Council passed Resolution (UNSC) 1970, suspending Libya from the UN Human Rights Council, implementing sanctions, and calling for an International Criminal Court (ICC) investigation into the killing of unarmed civilians, a national matter, changing the regime and constitutions turned International and the National Transitional (NTC) Council of Libya, an executive board, was formed in March 2011 and was de facto assembled as an "executive team." When the NTC issued a Constitutional Declaration in August 2011 and set up a road map for the transition of the country to constitutional democracy with an elected government, it occupied the country's seat at the United Nations through gaining international recognition as the legitimate governing authority in Libya, i.e., unrecognition of the former constitution of the former government, overthrew the Libyan Arab Jamahiriya.

The sample of Libya and the UNSC intervention provides hints of the relation of constitutional law as a national matter within the sovereignty and international law and national law that physical borders are not the preventing separation of the national law and international law.

The Resolution 1970 (2011) expressed "grave concern" in Libya and condemned the use of force against civilians and condemned human rights repression and violations. Resolution 1970 (2011) contains a load of constitutional topics that are international law topics and relate to the constitution of the Libyan Arab Jamahiriya, e.g., the Resolution deplored the gross and systematic violation of human rights, including the repression of peaceful demonstrators (constitutional topic), expressing deep concern at the deaths of civilians, and rejecting the incitement unequivocally to hostility and violence against the civilian population made from the highest level of the Libyan government (constitutional topic to cite a government and its responsibility). Moreover, the Resolution underlined the need to respect the freedoms of peaceful assembly (constitutional topic) and expression (constitutional topic), including freedom of the media (constitutional topic).

In an international law document, providing and referencing constitutional topics led me to conclude a transnational relation between international law and national law in a geometric design.

Further, after the defense of my dissertation in 2019, another sample supporting the idea popped in 2020. The case of Venezuelan gold stored at the Bank of England led the high court of England to decide on to whom should the gold returns, the Guaidó Board or the Maduro Board, where both Boards were claiming to represent the legitimate government of Venezuela referring to the constitutional of Venezuela and simultaneously have international recognition.

The dissertation is now updated and abstracted to this manuscript and supports the idea to theoretically evaluate certain national legal phenomena from an international law point of view and spot transnational connections among them.

The purpose of this manuscript's main idea, i.e., evaluation of constitutions, is to find, connect, and address, drawing topics on a national constitution with international dimensions in another spectrum of geometric relations here called transnational.

This idea may help to understand other national phenomena, a revolution so that the international community can prevent violations of human rights in such a phenomenon more actively as what occurred in Libya after the Arabian Spring and engagement of the United Nations Security Council.

Is international law theoretically able to evaluate a violation of human rights, e.g., any threat to the peace and breach of the peace pre occurrence? in other words, Is a constitution evaluative by international law and human rights? In case affirmative, is it possible for an international subject to refer to any national constitution?

In this regard, transnational evaluation refers to a theoretical method of collecting and comparing ostensibly normative international law and human rights in the constitutions. The proposed method argues a model of evaluation to classify and rate the constitutions through comparative standards in the conjunction of international law and human rights merits.

The manuscript also discusses international law and human rights normative effects on constitutions. It provides pieces of evidence of international law and human rights used in recently amended constitutions and references for either direct or indirect (vernacularized) international and human rights terms in the constitutions. Finally, it elaborates a method of evaluation and applies its method to a group of selected constitutions.

As a result, this book suggests a method that uses legal informatics of constitutional texts to automate and mechanize legal analysis and designed an evaluation method that connects traditional subjects of international law and constitutional topics transnationally.

Xi'an, China Ali Shirvani

Acknowledgments Many thanks to my family, and supportive supervisor, professor Cai CongYan. I also extend gratitude to my colleague, professor Wang Jin at the Institution of Middle Eastern Studies, Northwest University.

Introduction

Principles of international law (IL) along with human rights (HR) standards are increasingly vernacularized in national legislation. Since the foundation of the United Nations (1945) and the adoption of the Universal Declaration of Human Rights (UDHR-1948), they are not only updated but also mainly are growing normatively. HR standards are literally used afterward in the most important national legal documents, i.e., constitutions.

Newly written constitutions and amended constitutions are more providing explicit references to provisions relating to the fundamental rights, and liberties recognized IL treaties that shall be construed in conformity with the UDHR and international treaties and agreements thereon ratified, e.g., the Constitution of Portugal promulgated in 1976, revised in 2005, article 16 states: "The provisions of this Constitution and laws concerning fundamental rights shall be interpreted and construed in accordance with the Universal Declaration of Human Rights." or article 7 of the Constitution of the Islamic Republic of Afghanistan declares: "The state shall observe the United Nations Charter, interstate agreements, as well as international treaties to which Afghanistan has joined, and the Universal Declaration of Human Rights. The state shall prevent all kinds of terrorist activities, cultivation and smuggling of narcotics, and production and use of intoxicants."

Many constitutions have drafted and promulgated before the establishment of the United Nations (1945). However, almost all of them faced amendments afterward while trying explicit references to IL and human rights contexts.

Statistically, in the late 1990s, more than half of the current constitutions came into force. The proportion was up to a third in the twenty-first century. The number of amendments is increasing periodically. These newly amended constitutions face international law normative updates and their antecedent states' obligations of incorporated human rights. International law and human rights are making a significant contribution to the conceptual and contextual changes in constitutions. In this regard, this proposal tries to elaborate a method of classification of the constitution and its evaluation by international law and human rights norms. It also tries to extract common international law and human rights values to classify constitutions first and then render the extracted values as a sample evaluation index.

Contents

About the Author

Dr. Ali Shirvani is currently an associate professor at the School of Oriental and African Studies of Xi'an International Studies University and a non-resident fellow at the Center for China and Globalization (CCG), P. R. China. Ali studied law at the University of Isfahan and graduated in international law from Xiamen University. He was a research fellow at the Institute of Middle Eastern Studies, Northwest University, Xi'an. His research areas are the conjunctions of international law and constitutional law, where he focused on common standards and comparative norms of constitutions from a transnational perspective. He suggests using legal informatics of constitutional texts to automate, compute, and mechanize legal analysis in his works.

He works on classification methods and, consequently, evaluating constitutions through the prism of international law and human rights values. He is also the founder and editor of the blog constitutional law in Persian producing updated pieces of constitutional latest constitutional matters worldwide as a feed for researchers of the Persian language field. He has written several essays in related areas and translated articles published as a book, Private Law beyond Nation State (Studies on the globalization and Europeanization of private law) with Alireza Arvahi, a selection of essays from Jürgen Basedow.

Acronyms

ACHPR	African Charter on Human and Peoples' Rights and Protocols
ACHR	American Convention on Human Rights
ACHR2	Arab Charter on Human Right
ADHPR	African Declaration of Human and People's Rights
CEDAW	Convention on the Elimination of all Forms of Discrimination against Women
CESCR	Committee on Economic, Social, and Cultural Rights
CL	Constitutional Law
CR	Constitutional Rights
CRC	Convention on the Rights of the Child
CRPD	Convention on the Rights of Persons with Disabilities
ECHR	European Convention on Human Rights
ECtHR	European Court of Human Rights
FR	Fundamental Rights
HR	Human Rights
HRC	Human Rights Council
IACHR	Inter-American Court of Human Rights
ICCPR	International Covenant on Civil and Political Rights
ICCPR-OP1	Optional Protocol to the International Covenant on Civil and Political Rights
ICCPR-OP2	Second Optional Protocol to the International Covenant on Civil and Political Rights, aiming at the abolition of the death penalty
ICERD	International Convention on the Elimination of All Forms of Racial Discrimination
ICESCR	International Covenant on Economic, Social, and Cultural Rights
ICMW	International Convention on the Protection of the Rights of All Migrant Workers and Members of Their Families
IL	International Law
IO	International Organizations
NGO	Non-Governmental Organization
NL	National Law

OHCHR	Office of the High Commissioner for Human Rights
UDHR	Universal Declaration of Human Rights
UN	United Nations
UNACT	Convention Against Torture and Other Cruel, Inhuman or Degrading Treatment or Punishment
UNGA	United Nations General Assembly
UNGEGN	United Nations Group of Experts on Geographical Names
UNHCHR	United Nations High Commissioner for Human Rights
UNHCR	United Nations High Commissioner for Refugees
UNICEF	United Nations Children's Fund
UNSC	United Nations Security Council
VDPA	The Vienna Declaration and Programme of Action
WCHRV	World Conference on Human Rights in Vienna 1993

Abbreviations

ACDMCFRRGHT	Right to Academic Freedom
AMPRRGHT	Right to Amparo
APLJDCLDCSNRGHT	Right to Appeal Judicial Decisions
ARMSRGHT	Right to Bear Arms
BCHMB	Both Chambers of the Legislature
BSNSRGHT	Right to Establish a Business
CHLDRGHT	Rights of Children
CLTRRGHT	Right to Culture
CNSLRGHT	Right to Counsel
CNTRY	The Formal Name of the Country in the Constitution
CSTINTLW	Constitutional References to Customary International Law
CTRNCRGHT	Right to Renounce Citizenship
DBTRSRGHT	Rights of Debtors
DCTTL	Title of the Document
DGNT	Human Dignity
DVLPRSNLTRGHT	Right to Development of Personality
ENDRNC	Period Since the Latest Changes Including Amendments
EXMWTRGHT	Right to Examine Evidence/Witnesses
FCHMB	First (or only) Chamber
FNDFAMRGHT	Right to Found a Family
FRMRKTRGHT	Right to a Competitive Marketplace
FRNINVST	References to Foreign Investment/Foreign Capital
FRNTRD	References to Foreign or International Trade
FRTRLRGHT	Right to a Fair Trial
GVN/CBNT	The Government/Cabinet
HDFRNAFRS	The Representative of the State for Foreign Affairs
HDG	Head of Government
HDS	Head of State
HLTHCRRGHT	Right to Health Care
HRGHTCMSN	Human Rights Commission

INALRGHT	Inalienable Rights
INFRGHT	Right to Information
INTLW	References to International law
INTORGS	References to International organizations
INTRGHT	Reference to Human Rights Treaties/Instruments
INTRTCNT	Status of the International Treaties, Superior/Inferior
INTTRT	References to International Treaties
JRTRL	Jury Trials Required
JUDCRTS3	Establishment of courts of Amparo
LCL	Left Explicitly to non-CL the Legislature
LFE	Right to Life
LIBELRGHT	Right to Protect One's Reputation
LISRRGHT	Right to Rest/leisure
MDL	References to a Model or Ideal
MRGRGHT	Right to Marry
NEXPLN	Answer to the Inquiry Needs Explanations
NOMILRGHT	Right to Conscientious Objection
NSPCFD	Answer to the Inquiry is Unascertained or not Specified
OCPTNRGHT	Right to Choose an Occupation
OMBDS	Ombudsman
OVRTHRRGHT	Right to Overthrow the Government
PBTRLRGHT	Right to Public Trial
PROPRGHT	Right to Own Property
PRTRLRGHT	Right to Pre-trial Release
PRVCRGHT	Right to Privacy
PTNRGHT	Right of the Petition
RMNRRGHT	Right to Equal Pay for Work
SCHMB	Second Chamber of the Legislature
SHLTRRGHT	Right to Shelter
SLFDTMNRGHT	Right to Self-determination
SPDTRLRGHT	Right to Speedy Trial
STANDLIV	Right to a Reasonable Standard of Living
STRIKRGHT	Right to Strike
SVRNGT	The Sovereignty, the People/State/Nation
TESTATERGHT	Right to Transfer Property Freely after Death
TRLLNG	Trial in the Native Language
TRNSFRPRPRGHT	Right to Transfer Property
UDTRMNBL	Answer to the Inquiry is Undeterminable
WRKRGHT	Right to Work

List of Figures

Chapter 1
Revolutions, National Constitutions Changes, and the Challenges of International Law

Abstract International law and human rights obligations and norms are growing universally by states practice and consent, especially in national legislation and smoothly constitution. Principles of international law and human rights obligations are increasingly adopted in national legislation. Since the foundation of the United Nations (1945) and adoption of the Universal Declaration of Human Rights (1948), subjects such as state, sovereignty, humankind, and rights have been keeping updating and upgrading from conceptual and contextual perspectives. However, the fact is that most constitutions were promulgated before the establishment of United Nations (1945), while many of them have been updated (amended) after that. Statistically, in the late 1990s, more than half of the current constitutions came into force. The proportion was up to a third in the twenty-first century. The number of amendments is increasing periodically. These newly amended constitutions are not only facing international law normative updates but also their antecedent states' obligations of incorporated human rights. International law and human rights are making a significant contribution to the conceptual and contextual changes in constitutions. While constitutions are the national matters, consequently public law, the question is the possibility of classification and evaluation of constitutions by international law and human rights at the first stage. The second question is the connection of two different fields of law, i.e., international law and constitutional law; the hypothesis approximates the two through the comparative, transnational approach and use of standard ground connections. Scrutiny of the updated constitutions which are affected by international obligations and norms, improves the rule of law and good governance by shedding light on public law dimensional sphere which is a gap from a common point of international and constitutional law view. This study is trying to find common international law and human rights values for classification of constitutions and rendering the extracted values as a sample evaluation index.

A. Shirvani, *Transnational Evaluation of Constitutions*, SpringerBriefs in Law,
https://doi.org/10.1007/978-981-16-2976-1_1

1.1 Calling International Law and Human Rights in Recent National Revolutions

While the world is changing rapidly, and there are increasing calls for international legal responses in areas such as globalization, development, democratization, and technology, Arab-Spring had shown the new serial emergence of hard way changes of the constitution under human rights (HR) violation and international law (IL) considerations. Occurred revolutions in the Middle East and North Africa (MENA), named Arab-Spring,[1] had caused more need for active IL reaction and use of legal solutions.[2] Although they are a series of national phenomenon, they engaged the United Nations (UN) and its bodies,[3] and some even caused continuous UN Security Council (UNSC) resolutions in various aspects. On one side, national episodes of the consecutive wave of leaders fall, failed states, constitutional changes, civil wars, began by surprising Jasmine Revolution in the Republic of Tunisia continued in Egypt, Yemen, Libya, and the longest in the Syrian Arab Republic. On the other side, IL and HR violations geared up public IL scholars more than before.[4] From Tunisia as the first to Syria, which is the longest and might not be the last, IL and HR engagement, there seems a need for International legal solutions to prevent or reduce such violations. What and how that would be the shape of a legal, here IL and HR approach to avoid them, is the hypothesis which this dissertation tries to elaborate and will come below; in this chapter, after a short review of recent Arabian spring revolutions (subtitle 1–5) there is a linkage between the joint list of international commitments of the states faced revolution and the result of hard changes of constitutions (subtitle 6), part two and three talks about the primary and sub-question of the dissertation base and tries to visualize connections between IL and HR normative improvements and recent constitutional changes which might use as a foundation of analyzation and classification; and at last part four and five of this chapter, justifies this research and discusses the methodology of research. Arab Spring, in particular, shows the need for seeking evaluation of constitutions for precaution of hard way change of constitutions. Here is a short review of recent revolutions and the engagement of IL and HR.

---

[1]Republic of Tunisia, Arab Republic of Egypt, Libya, Syrian Arab Republic, Republic of Yemen, Kingdon of Saudi Arabia, Republic of Iraq, State of Kuwait, Kingdom of Bahrain, Hashemite Kingdom of Jordan, Kingdom of Morocco, Sultanate of Oman, Republic of the Sudan, Islamic Republic of Mauritania, Republic of Djibouti and Federal Republic of Somalia.

[2]Marc Lynch, *The Arab Uprisings Explained: New Contentious Politics in the Middle East*, Columbia studies in Middle East politics (New York: Columbia University Press, 2014). P22.

[3]Oliver C. Ruppel, Kathrin M. Scherr, and Alexander D. Berndt (Ed), *Assessing Progress in the Implementation of Zimbabwe's New Constitution: National, Regional and Global Perspectives*, Recht und Verfassung in Afrika—Law and Constitution in Africa (Deutschland: NOMOS, 2017). P84.

[4]David Armstrong, *Routledge Handbook of International Law*, ed. Jutta Brunée et al. (Oxon: Routledge, 2009). P184.

1.1.1 *International Law and the Arab Spring Revolution*

(1) ***Tunisia***

The story began with the self-immolation of a Tunisian citizen who was a young vegetable cart owner in December 2010, whose act ignited a revolution and months of protests, finally caused 23 years old regime of President Ben Ali in January 2011[5]; however, the Tunisian revolution and protest have not so many and ***HR and fundamental rights (FR)*** violation. UN Secretary-General Ban Ki-moon said: "…every effort must be made by all concerned parties to establish dialogue and resolve problems peacefully to prevent further loss, violence, and escalations."[6]

(2) ***Egypt***

Following Tunisian people victory against their regime, the same protest started on 25th January 2011 in Cairo; since the Office of the United Nations High Commissioner for Human Rights (OHCHR) was monitoring the HR situation, it asked national authorities to refrain from the use of violence and to respect people's FR to demonstrate peacefully. OHCHR recommends full respect for ***international HR norms*** that can be secured, in particular by the lifting of the state of emergency in place since 1981; It recommends enjoyment of Egyptian people from full *freedom of expression, freedom of assembly* which may know as ***constitutional rights (CR)*** than HR.[7] Even after Hosni Mobarak's removal and drafting a new constitution in 2012, The UN HR chief voiced alarm at a rising tension; she also mentioned deaths and injuries during protests related to the draft constitution while drawing specific attention to several problems with the text.[8]

(3) ***Yemen***

The revolution started simultaneously with the Egyptian revolution on 27 January 2011 in Capital Sana' and soon faced international reactions; The Secretary-General and three independent UN HR experts strongly condemned attacks on peaceful protesters. Ban Ki-moon deeply troubled by the continuing violence and instabilities, and Independent UN HR experts condemned the government crackdown and urged authorities to stop the excessive use of force to end protests.In a joint statement, Christof Heyns, the Special Rapporteur on extrajudicial executions, described the attacks against peaceful demonstrators as "***a clear violation of international law***."Frank La Rue, the Special Rapporteur on freedom of opinion and expression, noted that any government's role is to serve its people. "This means allowing them

[5]"Constitutional history of Tunisia," International IDEA accessed 15 Jan, 2017, http://www.constitutionnet.org/country/constitutional-history-tunisia.

[6]"In quotes: Reaction to Tunisian crisis," BBC News Services, 2011, accessed 18 Nov, 2013, http://www.bbc.com/news/world-africa-12197681.

[7]"Report of the OHCHR Mission to Egypt 27 March–4 April 2011," 2011, accessed 13 Nov, 2013, http://www.ohchr.org/Documents/Countries/EG/OHCHR_MissiontoEgypt27March_4April.pdf.

[8]"UN official voices alarm at Egypt violence, cites 'major' problems with draft constitution," 2012, accessed 7 Jan, 2013, http://www.un.org/apps/news/story.asp?NewsID=43706.

to express their grievances peacefully, listening to, and effectively addressing such concerns." Juan Méndez, the Special Rapporteur on torture, voiced his alarm at seeing images showing security personnel using excessive force against protesters. "It is indeed a worrying trend when States use violence and excessive force to try to end long-standing grievances which, ironically, also include ***accusations of serious human rights violations*** such as police brutality and torture."[9]

(4) ***Libya***

Following the epidemic Arab-Spring in the region, a ***civil war*** initiated in early 2011; The opponents of president Gaddafi formed a committee named the *National Transitional Council* to act as an interim authority on 27 February 2011, the government began an armed conflict with them, which caused UNSC Approves 'No-Fly Zone' over Libya, which authorized 'All Necessary Measures' to Protect Civilians. "Demanding an immediate ceasefire in Libya, including an end to the current attacks against civilians, which it said might constitute "**crimes against humanity**," the Security Council this evening imposed a ban on all flights in the country's airspace—a no-fly zone—and tightened sanctions on the Qadhafi regime and its supporters."[10] The resolution 1973 (2011) authorized UN member states, acting nationally, to take all necessary measures to protect the ***people of Libya*** from their president, who were under threat of attack in the country, especially in Benghazi, the capital. The resolution also mentioned the vital role of the **League of Arab States (LAS)** in the achievements of international peace and security in the region, and bearing in mind the UN Charter's Chapter VIII,[11] the Council asked the League's members to cooperate with other states.

(5) ***Syria***

Inspired by similar events across the region, on 26 January 2011, protests began against Syria's ruling regime and soon turned into an ongoing civil war and international crises after president Bashar al-Assad violently repressed a revolt.[12] Soon later on April 2011, after UNSC briefed by the Under-Secretary-General for Political Affairs and the Human Rights Council (HRC), adopted a resolution at its seventeenth special session (S-17/1. Situation of human rights in the Syrian Arab Republic) reaffirmed the purposes and principles of the Charter, the Universal Declaration of Human Rights (UDHR), and relevant International HR treaties, especially article 4 the International Covenant on Civil and Political Rights (ICCPR) and that all States

[9]"Secretary-General deplores killing of Yemeni protesters by security forces," updated 18 March 2011, 2011, accessed 18 Nov, 2013, http://www.un.org/apps/news/story.asp?NewsID=37811.

[10]"Resolution SC/10200 17 MARCH 2011," 2011, accessed 16 May, 2016, https://www.un.org/press/en/2011/sc10200.doc.htm.

[11]Which hold: "…Encourage the development of pacific settlement of local disputes through such regional arrangements or by such regional agencies either on the initiative of the states concerned or by reference from the Security Council."

[12]For more details on the chronology of Syria crises: "Chronology of Events," updated 2 February 2017, 2011, accessed 18 Jan, 2017, http://www.securitycouncilreport.org/chronology/syria.php?page=6.

are bound to promote and protect HR and fundamental freedoms, requested an investigative mission to Syria.[13] Until now, 13 SC resolutions mostly unanimously adopted about Syrian civil war, access to humanitarian aid, and related issues.[14]

1.1.2 International Commitments of Arab Spring States

Constitutional changes along with HR violations happened in these revolutions, while the people were looking for their rights or more in comparison, these countries and their sovereign states have had IL and HR commonalities before which could have served to them such as:

(1) They are all members of the UN charter.
(2) They are all members of the League of Arab States (LAS http://www.lasportal.org/).
(3) They are all members of the Organisation of Islamic Cooperation (OIC http://www.oic-oci.org/).
(4) They are all members of the Cairo Declaration on Human Rights in Islam (CDHRI).
(5) Shari'ah is the primary source of their constitutions.
(6) Islam is their most official religion.

Add to it their constitutional approach to IL and treaties might be common and needs comparative analysis. In this regard, it was possible if their IL and HR commitments have been fulfilled or measured, or their lack, the revolution could have been avoided.

Although in different layer and topic, two below commons in indexes implies the above theory:

(7) All regimes ranked authoritarian or hybrid regimes.[15]
(8) Relative ranking on the rule of law indexes (Figs. 1.1 and 1.2).

[13] "Situation of human Rights in the Syrian Arab Republic," 2011, accessed 18 March, 2014, http://www.ohchr.org/EN/HRBodies/HRC/SpecialSessions/Session17/Pages/17thSpecialSession.aspx.

[14] For more UN documents about Syrian civil war: "UN Documents for Syria," accessed 8 Apr, 2016, http://www.securitycouncilreport.org/un-documents/syria/.

[15] The Economist Intelligence Unit's Democracy Index, "The Economist Democracy Index" (London: The Economist 2016). https://infographics.economist.com/2017/DemocracyIndex/.

TUNISIA

Tunis, Sfax, Sousse

1. WJP Rule of Law Index

Income
Upper middle
Region
Middle East & North Africa
Population
11m (2012)
66% Urban
27% in three largest cities

WJP RULE OF LAW INDEX FACTORS		SCORE	GLOBAL RANKING	REGIONAL RANKING	INCOME GROUP RANKING
Factor 1:	Limited Government Powers	0.58	41/97	2/7	9/30
Factor 2:	Absence of Corruption	0.52	39/97	3/7	9/30
Factor 3:	Order and Security	0.79	31/97	2/7	3/30
Factor 4:	Fundamental Rights	0.56	63/97	2/7	20/30
Factor 5:	Open Government	0.46	55/97	4/7	18/30
Factor 6:	Regulatory Enforcement	0.55	38/97	3/7	8/30
Factor 7:	Civil Justice	0.56	42/97	4/7	10/30
Factor 8:	Criminal Justice	0.52	43/97	2/7	10/30

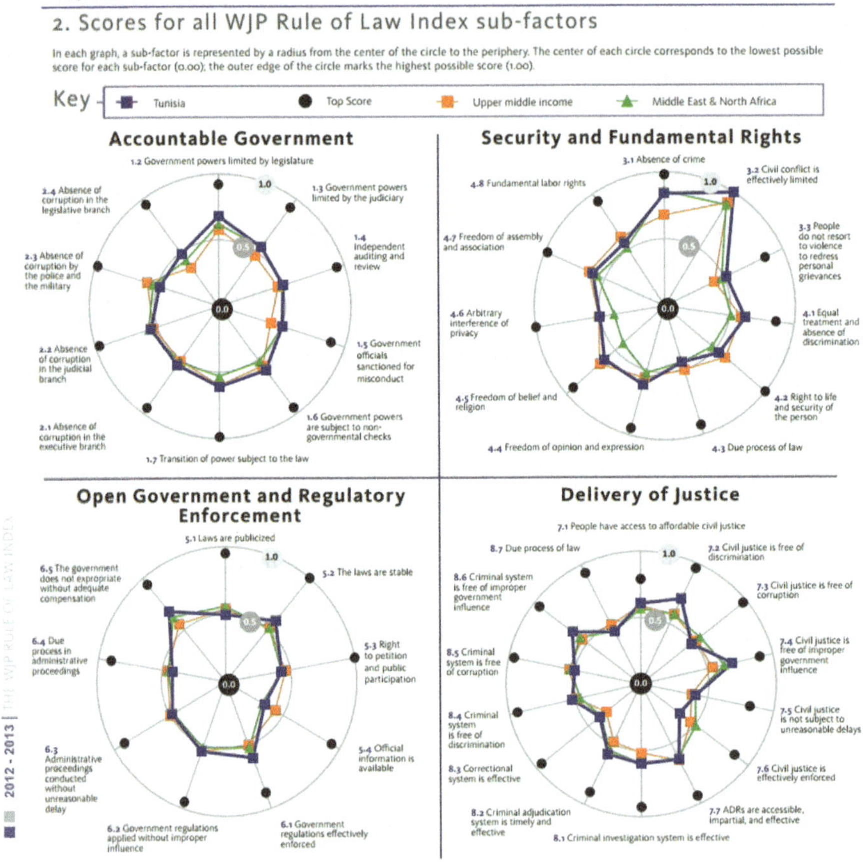

Fig. 1.1 Tunisia rule of law index in 2012–13[16]

[16]World Justice Project, "Rule of Law Index" (Washington, D.C., 2012–13). https://worldjusticeproject.org/our-work/publications/rule-law-index-reports/wjp-rule-law-index-2012-2013-report. P144.

EGYPT

Cairo, Alexandria, Giza

1. WJP Rule of Law Index

Income
Lower middle

Region
Middle East & North Africa

Population
84m (2012)
44% Urban
31% in three largest cities

WJP RULE OF LAW INDEX FACTORS		SCORE	GLOBAL RANKING	REGIONAL RANKING	INCOME GROUP RANKING
Factor 1:	Limited Government Powers	0.58	40/97	1/7	3/23
Factor 2:	Absence of Corruption	0.51	41/97	4/7	2/23
Factor 3:	Order and Security	0.67	65/97	7/7	12/23
Factor 4:	Fundamental Rights	0.43	89/97	6/7	19/23
Factor 5:	Open Government	0.48	51/97	2/7	5/23
Factor 6:	Regulatory Enforcement	0.42	77/97	6/7	14/23
Factor 7:	Civil Justice	0.47	73/97	6/7	13/23
Factor 8:	Criminal Justice	0.45	56/97	5/7	6/23

2. Scores for all WJP Rule of Law Index sub-factors

In each graph, a sub-factor is represented by a radius from the center of the circle to the periphery. The center of each circle corresponds to the lowest possible score for each sub-factor (0.00); the outer edge of the circle marks the highest possible score (1.00).

Key: Egypt; Top Score; Lower middle income; Middle East & North Africa

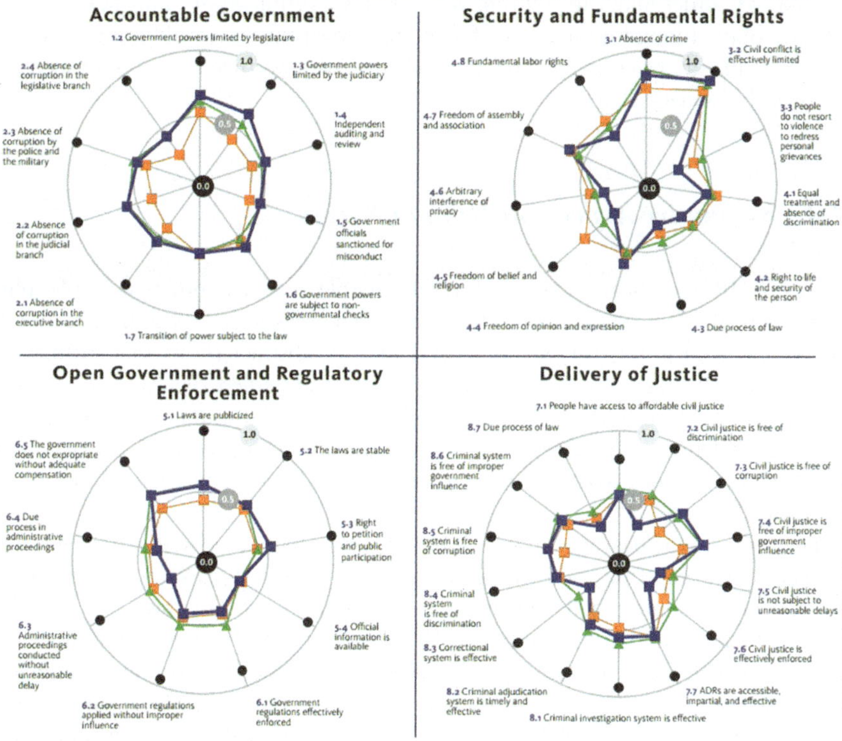

COUNTRY PROFILES | EGYPT

Fig. 1.2 Egypt rule of law index in 2012–13[17]

[17] Project, "Rule of Law Index." P85.

1.1.3 Venezuela and Lima Group

The Foreign Ministers and Representatives of 12 South American states plus Canada,[18] on 8 August 2017, addressed Venezuela's critical situation and signed a declaration, established an international organization to search mechanisms for the contribution of democracy in Venezuela through IL HR, peaceful and negotiated solution. They referenced the spirit of solidarity that characterized the region and the conviction that negotiation, with full respect for the norms of IL and the principle of nonintervention, does not violate HR and democracy, as an endurance solution to the differences; The Lima Group demands many constitutional issues at first glance looks business for IL however constitutional too, e.g., offers humanitarian aid, calls for free elections the release of prisoners who are political ones, and criticizes the breakdown of democratic order under the current Bolivarian Government of Venezuela.

This group's foreign ministers had said their governments would not accept Mr. Nicolas Maduro as the country's president when he was sworn in for a second six-year term in early January 2019.[19]

1.1.4 Normative Aspects of Human Rights

Updates in HR classifications made several possible analysis options possible, plus tracing them in other contents and documents. The reason is they are, first, moral, second, universal, third, fundamental, and, fourth, abstract rights that, fifth, take priority over all other norms.[20] Sometimes HR is classified regarding those that are fundamental or not, those that are violable or not, those that are collective or individual, and those that are justiciable or the opposite. Some types of classifications even go as far as categorizing HR regarding those which are procedural and those that are substantive.

There are various passages in which HR is traditionally classified. However, that classifying HR could be used as an instrument to encourages critical analysis in the intellectual inquiry of the meaning also in purpose of HR, and one can say, any classification of HR inevitably drives to problems, including the fact that it is inconsistent with the principles of indivisibility, universality, and interdependence of HR. At this moment for constitutional evaluation, the principle of universality plays the most critical role, and, in this hypothesis, it is essential to understand some

---

[18]Argentina **Republic, Federative Republic of** Brazil, **Republic of** Chile, **Republic of Colombia, Republic of** Costa Rica, **Republic of** Guatemala, **Republic of** Honduras, **United Mexican States, Republic of** Panama, **Republic of** Paraguay and **Republic of** Peru, **Co-operative Republic of** Guyana and **Saint Lucia** joined later.

[19]"Lima Group countries say won't recognize new Maduro mandate," January 05, 2019, accessed January 07, 2019, https://www.rappler.com/world/regions/latin-america/220338-lima-group-non-recognition-maduro.

[20]Michel Rosenfeld and András Sajó, *The Oxford Handbook of Comparative Constitutional Law* (Great Britain: Oxford University Press, 2012). P270.

elements of classifications and define the compatibility of constitutional rights to them.[21]

1.1.4.1 The Universality of Human Rights

In the past years, the principle of universality has become central to the interpretation of HR. The recognition and later the protection of fundamental rights (FR) to some extent been codified before the Second World War, primarily in national law and especially in constitutions. However, after World War two, politicians and civil society alike realized that national schemes for the protection of HR did not suffice. Since then, HR have found their way into a wide range of regional and global treaties.

The UN Charter entry to force on 24 October 1945 identified the formal recognition of HR as a universal principle, and compliance with HR declared in the Preamble, Arts 55 and 56 as a principle to be supported by all international actors, here states. Later consequently and subsequently followed by the adoption of additional international instruments discussed in chapter three. The UDHR stipulates over thirty rights and regards their protection; a general standard ultimately needs to be achieved. Several governments and scholars maintain that some HR in the UDHR has the character of jus cogens.[22]

The universality hinted through the fact that the document has been agreed upon in various states of the west and east with different international points of view. Western countries and some other countries such as the People Republic of China, the former Soviet Union, Chile, and Lebanon signed it. Moreover, this instrument was adopted with no objections and no votes against; only eight abstentions.

More countries turned independent and joined the UN, consequently endorsing this principle and its ideals. Such a commitment hinted in the 1968 Proclamation of Teheran, which was adopted by 85 states that more than 60 of the countries were not placed Western classification of countries. It states a common understanding of the countries' peoples concerning the inalienable and inviolable rights of all human family and constitutes an obligation for the international community's countries. The endorsement continued by The Vienna Declaration and Programme of Action (VDPA), which its conference attended by 171 states, underlined the importance of the UDHR and stated that the UDHR 'constitutes a common standard of accomplishment for all human beings and all their nations.

The universality is still a subject of intense deliberation, including in the forecast of other conferences. The Vienna document states that the universal nature of HR is 'beyond question.' It grants that all HR is universal. However, the significance

---

[21] "Spotlights on Health And Rights History and Categories of Human Rights," The Heilbrunn Department of Population and Family Health Columbia University, accessed 10 Mar, 2016, http://healthandrights.ccnmtl.columbia.edu/human_rights/history_categories_human_rights.html.

[22] A peremptory norm, which states are not allowed to derogate from; a rule which is considered universally valid.

of national and regional specifications and various historical, cultural, and religious backgrounds must be taken into judgment.[23]

The GA states UDHR as a general standard of achievement for all the people in all constitutions; in a way that every individual and every organ of the international society, keeping the UDHR always in judgment. It shall endeavor by teaching and education to promote respect for the rights and freedoms mentioned, and through national and international, progressive measures secures their universal and sufficient recognition and practice, both between the peoples of member states and the peoples of territories under their jurisdiction. Art 1: All human beings are born free and equal in dignity and their rights. They are enriched with reason and conscience and shall run towards one another in the sense of brotherhood. The predicament is that the UDHR engages universalist rhetoric in presenting a particular position, that of the liberal rights tradition. Such a position is normatively universal. However, it is not shared universally by all human persons and the traditions and societies in which they live in.[24]

HR differs from other rights in two respects. Firstly, they are characterized by being (a) Inherent in all human beings by their humanity; (b) Inalienable; and (c) Equally applicable to all. Secondly, the primary duties deriving from HR fall on states and their authorities or agents, not on individuals.

A significant implication of these characteristics is that HR needs protection via the rule of law. Besides, any arguments about rights should be submitted for adjudication through a sufficient, unprejudiced, and independent bench, applying procedures to ensure full equality and fairness to all the parties, and determining the question under specific, precise, and pre-existing laws, openly declared to the public and known for it.

The idea of basic rights arose from the necessity of protecting individuals against the autocratic use of power with the states. Therefore, the attention was concentrated initially on those rights which oblige states to refrain from particular actions. In this category, HR is generally referred to as 'fundamental freedoms.' As HR is viewed as a precondition for leading a dignified human existence, they serve as a guide and touchstone for legislation.

The vertical effect of rights refers to the individual-state relationship. Since the specific nature of HR, as an essential precondition for human development, hints in two relations, first that they can have a bearing on relations between the individual and the state and second between individuals themselves. The primary purpose of HR is to establish the rules adjusting the relations between the individual and the state. This so-called 'horizontal effect' implies, among other things, that a government not only must refrain from violating HR but also must protect the individual from infringements by other individuals.

---

[23]"Definitions and Classifications," Icelandic Human Rights Center, accessed 10 Mar, 2016, http://www.humanrights.is/en/human-rights-education-project/human-rights-concepts-ideas-and-fora/part-i-the-concept-of-human-rights/definitions-and-classifications.

[24]Michael E. Goodhart, *Human rights: politics and practice*, Third edition. ed. (Oxford; New York, NY: Oxford University Press, 2016). P11–26.

After the World Wars subsequently, the achievements of constitutional judicial review, one demanding CR model had remarkable success, first in Europe and world-wide. This model is characterized by a wide passageway to the scope of rights, which sometimes referred to as 'rights inflation,' the acceptance of horizontal impression of rights, not only positive obligations, but also increasingly socio-economic rights, and the use of the doctrines of balancing and proportionality to determine the permissible limitations of rights.[25]

However, national constitutions have, especially in the recent decades, been intensely shaped by IL; many constitutional actors, especially constitutional courts, are rejecting IL's claim to supremacy over domestic CL.

1.1.4.2 Normative Aspects of Human Rights

OHCHR has published a Guide to Measurement and Implementation HR called Indicators. It aims to develop indicators to measure progress in implementing international HR normative effects and their principles. The Guide tries to illustrate the conceptual and methodological framework for the indicators recommended by international and national HR mechanisms, and not only non-governmental organizations have used them but also a growing number of states. The guide provides concrete patterns of indicators identified for some HR—all originating from the UDHR—and some practical tools and models to promote the realization of HR at several layers. It attracted HR advocates as well as policymakers, development practitioners, statisticians, and others who are working to make HR. In order t to respond to a longstanding demand to develop and expand appropriate statistical indicators in furthering the cause of HR, OHCHR has also developed a framework of indicators. The advice of the World Conference on Human Rights in Vienna (WCHRV) recommended the use and analysis of indicators. The reason provided was helping measure progress in HR, which followed by the principles of universality, implies these rights are, by definition, valid for all people; second, impartiality and third objectivity.

Moreover, cooperation to strengthen the capacity of member states in meeting their HR obligations. However, national governments are already applying this framework, national HR institutions, and non-governmental organizations worldwide, however not constitutionally yet. Although HR standards have been set in practically almost areas that touch on human dignity (DGNT), normative gaps and weaknesses still exist, such as constitutions; A lot remains to be done. New normative frameworks are needed in these areas, while in others, they must be elaborated and strengthened. The standard setting is a dynamic process that must respond to a rapidly changing global and challenges that come with new conditions.[26]

---

[25] Christoph Moellers, *The Three Branches A Comparative Model of Separation of Powers*, ed. Martin Loughlin, John P. McCormick, and Neil Walke, Oxford Constitutional Theory (Great Britain: Oxford University Press, 2013). P2.

[26] Makau W. Mutua, "Standard Setting in Human Rights Critique and Prognosis," *Human Rights Quarterly Buffalo Legal Studies Research Paper No. 2007-013* 29 (2007), http://ssrn.com/abstract=1010947. P619–620.

1.2 Classification and Evaluation of Constitutions

The question is the possibility of classification and evaluation of constitutions by IL and HR at the first stage. The second face of the problem is the connection of two different law fields, i.e., IL and CL; the hypothesis approximates the two through the comparative, transnational approach and use of standard ground connections.

1.2.1 Classification of Constitutions

Can a constitution be classified/evaluated by IL and HR? Are the HR violations through revolutions predictable by IL and HR? The national status of international HR norms within constitutions, and their settings is an old but continuing issue. On one side, globalization and internationalization as the foundations of progress are by tradition dependent on states acting coherently, and their objective and trend are to create a general permeability in the state structure and national sovereignty. On the other side, the modern progress of IL norms and HR indexes and simultaneously emergence of hard way changes of the constitution, i.e., revolutions, with its impacts on the international community, IL, and HR, initiate new ideas of possibility of theoretical awareness and precautions of such phenomenon by analyzation of constitutions through IL and HR instruments. An IL-based evaluation that can analyze the HR standards in constitutions and states as the bearer of their commitments is the base idea, although any state has its different type of constitution; since all have many commons in comparative view that is a linkage of transnational and IL. States as the subject of IL have HR responsibilities in their jurisdiction for IL objects. Here, an evaluation may define a method to better understand a constitution's statute through recognized, experienced comparative IL and HR norms. The main subject of this manuscript is how to elaborate a theoretic framework for the evaluation of constitutions.

1.2.2 Evaluation of Constitutions

How to evaluate a constitution through IL and HR? The sub-question in this regard is about the varieties of evaluation frameworks and partial evaluations. States accessions to more international and HR treaties and their active roles in IL events, new constitutions are more under effects of commitment to them as new ones, and related constitutional amendments are more under the effect of UN charter and HR documents that load HR standards willing for *the people*, which may call common constitutional principles of HR. The classification differs from A to D, showing proficiency, normality, lacks, and precautionary needs.

Such analytics shows the need for an inclusive survey of finding, comparing, analyzing, and classification under IL norms and HR standards to create a theoretical classification and evaluation of a constitution if their related constitutional legal order works appropriately and whether it needs soft change.

IL and HR normative approaches are now widely speeded and offer various new perspectives through which constitutions' concentration becomes possible; moreover, a comparative analysis becomes available for IL, HR, and CL scholars. For answering these questions, this paper elaborates the idea of looking for the possibility of a comparative analysis of constitutions through IL norms and HR standards to avoid the hard way changes of constitutions and create a transnational index of constitutional matters of change. The combined historical comparison of the constitutional theory and political analysis proposed thesis links together theory and comparative analysis to make a new method to evaluate international constitutional elements.[27] It examines two core instruments: constitutional approaches to IL and HR, quantity and quality, amount and numbers of compatible social, economic, cultural, and political rights of a constitution, and its insight to IL. After setting out a theoretical framework, it provides a theoretical method of constitutional evaluation by IL norms and HR standards to answer the above question. Answers to questions of why a constitution needs to be changed or reformed in most revolutions and why such changing is different from democratic international recognized ways, that accompanied by HR violations, may lead to a peaceful way of evaluation of constitution and methods of reforming for IL and HR norm is implied in this analysis.

The result would be a reference methodological tool that contains resources on the international and regional normative standards for constitutional analysis of HR at the national level. All results are floating within a broad framework of public law (PL) encompassing the full range of HR from civil and political to economic, social, and cultural rights and the different systems by which these standards have been adopted into national laws.

1.3 Constitutional Tendencies to International Law and Human Rights Indexation

Constitutions are under revision in the age that IL normative approaches to HR become more pervasive and going forward for raising awareness, assisting IL subjects, civil society organizations, and national institutions, a better, more comfortable, and more accurate analysis and legal interpretation.[28] Such a national phenomenon brought the idea about how modern developments of IL instruments and HR measures would improve the possibility to prevent HR violation and seek IL role at national levels.

[27] İlker Gökhan Şen, *Sovereignty Referendums in International and Constitutional Law* (Springer International Publishing, 2015). P50.

[28] Mutua, "Standard Setting in Human Rights Critique and Prognosis." P548.

Moreover, international ranks addressing legal issues going forward step by step in HR and day by day in related documents. As an instance, Standard-Setting is a method to assess the achievement or efficiency of an international instrument's content; it is used for classification and multidimensional analysis. E.g., a mandatory task for The Office of the United Nations High Commissioner for Human Rights (OHCHR).[29]

On the other hand, all recent revolutions brought more highlights and strain to constitutional law (CL)[30] aspects under IL scrutiny. However, at the very first steps, it seems that there is no or at least little relation among IL and revolutions, i.e., constitutional changes, ongoing lists of background demonstrates a large number of commonalities which needs a comparative and transnational study to unveil new interdisciplinary perspective, between IL and CL with the HR axels. To say short, as a national and regional phenomenon, the Jasmine Revolution challenges IL and HR instruments.

"HR frame the moral, shape the political, and distinguish the legal in places as local and diverse as the family, the school, the workplace, the community, the nation, and the State."[31] The 48/141 resolution of the General Assembly (GA) emphasizing the responsibilities of all States, in *conformity with the Charter* and the need to observe the UDHR first to promote and encourage respect for all HR and fundamental freedoms for all, without distinction as to race, sex, language or religion. Also, the second for the full implementation of the HR instruments, including the International Covenant on Civil and Political Rights (ICCPR), as well as the International Covenant on Economic, Social and Cultural Rights (ICESCR).[32]

The active state responsibility to HR depends predominantly on the strength of its national institutions. The UN HR treaty system's worth can best be measured by referencing its ability to encourage and cultivate national implementation of and compliance with international HR standards. "This is the only valid test of that system's relevance and effectiveness."[33]

---

[29]"To promote and protect the enjoyment and full realization, by all people, of all rights established in the Charter of the United Nations and in international human rights laws and treaties."

"Human Rights Indicators: A Guide to Measurement and Implementation" (The Office of the High Commissioner for Human Rights (OHCHR)). http://www.ohchr.org/EN/Issues/Indicators/Pages/documents.aspx.

[30]There are two constitutional law concepts: one applicable to the law of a nation state with a codified constitution, like the United States, and second applicable to the law of every nation state whether its constitution is or is not codified. Carl Wellman, *Constitutional rights—what they are and what they ought to be* (New York, NY: Springer Berlin Heidelberg, 2016). Publisher description https://www.loc.gov/catdir/enhancements/fy1615/2016937981-d.html.

Table of contents only https://www.loc.gov/catdir/enhancements/fy1615/2016937981-t.html. P13.

[31]Patrick Macklem, *The sovereignty of human rights* (Oxford UK; New York, NY: Oxford University Press, 2015). P1.

[32]The most significant embodiment of human rights standards. Mutua, "Standard Setting in Human Rights Critique and Prognosis." P554.

[33]Philip Alston and James Crawford, *The future of UN human rights treaty monitoring* (Cambridge; New York: Cambridge University Press, 2000). Sample text http://www.loc.gov/catdir/samples/cam032/99034665.html.

IL sources are becoming more effective in other fields while strengthening IL's penetration like rainwater circulating in the international community from clouds to ocean and mountains, sea, rivers, and lakes. There has been a significant influx of debates on constitutionalism in IL, sparked by various globalization processes. While IL sources can be found in constitutions,[34] its norms passed traditional IL boundaries and infiltrated domestic legislation. The dense connections of the international negotiation forums and enhanced possibilities of iterated interaction in the global realm increased the effectiveness of formalizing international norms through treaties and constitutional quality agreements. In the twentieth century, the renewed advent of globalization was marked by a far-reaching change in states' position and status and sovereign political actors. The rise in IL and HR's practical efficiency in local laws echoes the complexity of transformation that, in an admittedly decentralizing ambivalent direction, IL and CL are more interconnected than traditions. All manner of terms, ranging from the people, human, constitutional rights, HR, state, and sovereignty, has been engaged to explain increased interdependence, cooperation, and the need for more dimensional collaboration in the international, intranational, and transnational sphere.

Also, the research assesses the quality of specific international legal events from the perspective of their ability to respect and protect constitutionalist principles. It illustrates and justifies new institutions, mechanisms, and policies that might contribute to realizing better HR's objectives, in this regard normative analysis.

Constitutions have traditionally included references to foreign affairs and IL. Classic examples are constitutional clauses on state organs' powers in foreign affairs, especially about international treaties' conclusion. However, in recent decades, constitutional provisions relating to IL and international institutions have been significantly refined.

By improvements comparative constitutional law and movements of ideas, currently, constitutions are using more international legal concepts, nowadays they provide for the binding force of IL within the domestic sphere and sometimes explicitly and sweepingly recognize the primacy of IL over domestic law. Reference is made in many state constitutions to international organizations, especially to the UN.[35]

Constitutions also contain clauses on the state's accession to international organizations. In EU member states' constitutions, provision is made to transfer sovereign powers to the EU or the pooling of sovereignty within the EU. Most recently,

---

Publisher description http://www.loc.gov/catdir/description/cam0210/99034665.html.
Table of Contents http://lcweb.loc.gov/catdir/toc/99034665.html. P201.

[34] Rules recognized by constitutions, as evidence of a general practice arise from constitutions and general principles of law recognized by civilized nation's constitutions.

[35] Art. 28 of the Algerian Constitution of 19 November 1976, as amended on 28 November 1996: 'Algeria works for the reinforcement of international cooperation and to the development of friendly relations among states, on equal basis, mutual interest and noninterference in the internal affairs. It endorses the principles and objectives of the United Nations Charter.'

Fig. 1.3 Constitutions under normative pressure

clauses regarding the International Criminal Court (ICC), concerning its jurisdiction or surrender of persons to the Court, has been introduced.[36]

As it goes on, more than in the rights and liberties areas, there has been a "migration of constitutional ideas across legal systems, the rise of "constitutionalism beyond the state," or "transnational constitutionalism," and the formation of an Esperanto-like "generic" form of CL" (Fig. 1.3).[37]

1.3.1 Outsiders

A new form of constitutional interpretation by outsiders rather than constitutional institutions suggests an increasingly common phenomenon in a globalizing world may call outsider interpretation; e.g., it occurred in the context of constitutional contests in the past ten years in Fiji, Pakistan, Afghanistan, Honduras, and Nicaragua, and Zimbabwe. The distinct patterns of an outsider, or extra-territorial interpretation, also identifies in projects of comparative constitutional scholars, the judgments of constitutional courts with foreign constitutional subjects, and NGO's and IGO's in

[36] Art. 53-2 French Constitution (constitutional revision of 8 July 1999); Art. 16 (2), second sentence, German Basic Law (constitutional revision of 29 November 2000).

[37] Ran Hirschl, "Early Engagements with the Constitutive Laws of Others: Possible Lessons from Pre-Modern Religious Law," *Law & Ethics of Human Rights* 10, no. 1 (2016), https://doi.org/10.1515/lehr-2016-0003.

courts such as the US Supreme Court or the European Court of Human Rights.[38] Outsiders are producing new ways of interpretation and understandings. They are smoothly going to affect national constitutions' understanding in a comparative and multidimensional arena. Outsiders are new arrivals of globalization and cosmopolitanism; it might not be far that a foreign national reference to a constitution rather than his own country and request its application. The current constitution of **Germany 1949 (rev. 2014)** considers its people acknowledgment of the inviolable and inalienable HR as the basis of other communities, of peace and justice in the world. Therefore, not only foreign nationals may refer to it, but ECtHR can also interpret it and subsequently refer to its content.

1.3.2 Human Rights Standard-Setting

Standard setting in HR has been a contentious and mixed trend since the start of the HR movement. Not an easy task, standard setting is mixed by features of IL and national law when it concerns the provisions related to the government and the citizen, especially the limitation of state power and reaches versus the individual. States have traditionally viewed their power and authority over citizens as largely unlimited, which is why efforts to curb state power and impose red lines about what the state can and cannot do. While international institutions recommend democracy as the only legitimate form of the national government, globalization, especially on governance, has removed many issues from the domestic battlefield and citizens' political control. The multiplicity of religious and ethical approaches to the world that agree on a minimum of common values so important the emergence of an additional, more individualist basis for IL's legitimacy implies that IL does care about national constitutional standards.

In the HR discourse, rights provide the avenues through which DGNT is secured and guaranteed. The term implies duty and the bearer of it. In HR law, the state bears the primary duty of protecting rights, which individuals and groups enjoy, and a right seen as an entitlement.

Rights-based constitutional democracies, such as the EU member states and the ECHR members, recognize international constitutionalism and international courts as the necessary complements of societal constitutionalism to protect HR, democratic accountability, and the rule of law across frontiers. Constitutional democracies like the United States, which rely more on democratic processes than on substantive FR, sometimes perceive IL and intergovernmental organizations as a potential threat to national sovereignty.[39]

---

[38]"Another Dimension to Transnational Constitutionalism? Outsider Constitutional Interpretation," accessed 10 October 18 http://www.iconnectblog.com/2012/11/article-review-vicki-jackson-and-rosalind-dixon-on-outsider-constitutional-interpretation/.

[39]Christian Joerges and Ernst-Ulrich Petersmann, *Constitutionalism, Multilevel Trade Governance And Social Regulation*, Studies in International Trade Law (North America (US and Canada): Hart Publishing, 2006). P13.

Many view constitutional incorporations of international HR treaties as an effective way to enforce standard-setting domestically. There are three general theories of explanation of such incorporation:

(1) States constitutionalize treaty rights since they are authoritative empirical norms;
(2) States constitutionalize treaty rights since they demand constitutional incorporation;
(3) States only constitutionalize treaty rights in their interest domain, and such a treaty does not change the state's behavior. If the first norm-based explanation is working, the treaty rights should be emulated widely when the treaty enters into force, regardless of ratification. And if the second, law-based explanation is working, states should constitutionalize their treaty obligations upon ratification. If the third, interest-based explanation is working, there should be no impact of HR treaties on constitutional commitments.[40]

The HR move from standard-setting to effective implementation depends, in considerable measure, on the availability of appropriate means for evaluation. Both quantitative and qualitative indicators contain such essential means. Somehow the importance of indicators for the cognizance of HR is widely recognized and even enshrined in HR treaties, as in article 31 of the CRPD, but their use has not yet become systematic.

1.3.3 Evolution of National and International Legal Systems

National legal systems are turning more likely to provide treaties direct effect and hierarchical superiority over domestic law, which is consistent with a desire to ensure effective implementation. Courts refer to international treaties that have been ratified by parliaments as the state's duty for private international law subjects and rights providing. Simultaneously, national legal systems have steadily expanded the categories of treaties whose ratification requires prior legislative approval, thus expanding the role of national legislatures in international lawmaking.[41]

Some constitutional clauses enshrine international HR give them priority over domestic law; however, they have not instantaneously led to a satisfactory HR record in many countries, but good law which corresponds to international standards is a minimum condition for improvements.

The influence of the twentieth century's dramatic political transformations on comparative constitutionalism is self-evident. It is accepted that the prevalence of

[40]Mila Versteeg, "Law versus Norms The Impact of Human Rights Treaties on Constitutional Rights," *Virginia Public Law and Legal Theory Research* (2013).

[41]Pierre Hugues and Mila Versteeg, "International Law in National Legal Systems: An Empirical Investigation," *American Journal of International Law, Virginia Public Law and Legal Theory Research Paper No. 24* 109, no. July 2015 (2015). P468.

HR in the IL and CL of the past half-century is primarily attributable to the international community's disgust with World War II's horrors. Similarly, the distinct liberal tilt toward Western comparative constitutional discourse had a direct effect on new constitution-making. The sophisticated debates in comparative constitutional design and the rise of constitutional engineering are intimately related to overall decolonization processes, new state formation, which are named the third wave of democratization.[42]

1.3.4 Constitutionalization

Constitutionalization of IL in this discourse within IL describes the label for evolving an international order based on some general dual factors in this dissertation organizing principles such as state sovereignty and consensualism to international legal order. The discourse recognizes and has creatively appropriated principles and values of constitutionalism. Subjects of IL and also the new doctrines are improving the process of constitutionalization. In general terms, constitutionalization is the process by which a legal order goes from an ad hoc, decentralized and consent-based system to one where the legal form and process curtailed the remit of action of constituted power holders.[43]

The debate on constitutionalization bears from a great variety of meanings assigned to the key terms. Constitutionalization may use as a label for the development of an international order based on any organizing principles such as state sovereignty, territorial integrity, and consensualism to an international legal order which acknowledges and has creatively allocated importantly modified principles, institutions, and procedures of constitutionalism. In the course of constitutionalization, the migration of norms, cross-implantation, harmonization, and hybridization happens in multiple directions.[44]

The constitutionalization of IL is accompanied and constituted by the internationalization and globalization of state constitutions consisting of the influx of international precepts such as HR standards into national constitutional texts and case-law, which simultaneously brings about a horizontal convergence of national constitutional law.

Constitutionalization of IL in this discourse within IL describes the label for evolving an international order based on some general dual factors in this dissertation organizing principles such as state sovereignty and consensualism to international legal order.

---

[42]Ran Hirschl, *Comparative Matters The Renaissance of Comparative Constitutional Law* (New York: Oxford University Press, 2014). P80, 112–3.

[43]Aoife O'Donoghue, *Constitutionalism in Global Constitutionalisation* (United Kingdom: Cambridge University Press, 2014). P15.

[44]"Global Constitutionalism," accessed 06 Mar, 2016, http://www.mpil.de/en/pub/research/areas/public-international-law/global-constitutionalism.cfm.

1.3.5 Fragmentation and Constitutionalism

The decentralized fabrication of IL results from a central world legislator's deficiency produced functional fragmentation of IL. In contrast, political fragmentation originates from the domestic sphere when different government departments negotiate several different treaties, and different administrative authorities handled different culmination areas and then applied them. Fragmentation also brought a response to globalization. The global problems ranging from climate deterioration over migration and terrorism to the financial crisis have demanded more international and special regulation.[45]

1.3.6 The People or Human, Endonym and Exonym Concept of the People

While at one hand, the people are the first and most important mentioned subjects of Constitutions (Endonyms), they are named all humankind and are the subject of HR, i.e., citizens are the fountain of power in constitutions (Horizontal).[46]

On the other hand, states are the subjects of IL and bearers of commitments for HR and IL (Vertical). The people are hiring the state sovereignty via constitutions; states act as representatives of nations in the international arena in order of constitutions; in this regard, sources of power in IL back to people, states submit their will of people and commitments in the internal and external arena of nations. I.e., the constitution is a model and catalyzer of people's power from internal to the outer sphere. People are turning from Endonyms to Exonym.[47]

1.3.7 States and Constitutions Under Strain of International Legal Order and Human Rights

The strain of universal, international, and regional HR instruments on states and their structures is increasing by modern methods of rankings and is manifold. The expression of consent is, therefore, secondary and not strictly positive. As in all the terms of the law, it is considered a bilateral dialectic product between process and

---

[45]"Constitutional Fragments – On the Interaction of Constitutionalization and Fragmentation in International Law," Working Paper, Centre for Global Constitutionalism, University of St. Andrews, 2015, accessed 26 Mar, 2016, http://papers.ssrn.com/sol3/papers.cfm?abstract_id=2591370. P5.

[46]Alain Marciano and Randall G. Holcombe, *Constitutional mythologies: new perspectives on controlling the state*, Studies in public choice (New York: Springer, 2011). Table of contents only http://www.loc.gov/catdir/toc/fy12pdf01/2011934053.html. P4.

[47]P. R. Baehr, *Human rights: universality in practice* (New York, N.Y.: St. Martin's Press, 1999). Table of Contents http://lcweb.loc.gov/catdir/toc/98055203.html. P43.

principle.[48] Although, no evaluation tool comprehensively addresses the content of states constitutional approach to IL and HR. While there are nine core international HR instruments and around 1000 policy and operational indicators, such an evaluation framework may use as an asset in some ways, e.g., UN HR bodies and related organizations, or a reference to the minimum and maximum constitutional capacity of IL and HR.

IL has developed what many might consider a constitutional understanding of individual civil rights that individuals can claim vis-à-vis their governments. Globalization puts state constitutions under strain. Global problems compel states to cooperate within international organizations and through bilateral and multilateral treaties. What were typically governmental functions, such as guaranteeing human security, freedom, and equality, are in part transferred to "higher" levels. Moreover, non-state actors, acting within states or transnational, are increasingly entrusted with the exercise of traditional state functions. This led to exercised "governance" beyond the states' constitutional confines. Therefore, state constitutions can no longer comprehensively regulate the totality of governance, and the original claim of state constitutions to form a complete necessary order is defeated. National constitutions are, hollowed out, and traditional constitutional principles become dysfunctional or empty. The aforementioned affects the constitutional principle of democracy and the rule of law, the principle of social security, and the territory's organization. The traditional view of rights organizing relations between individuals and the state must give way to experiments and pragmatic governance across public and private sectors. Even those who drafted new constitutions must be open to the reinterpretation of their own words as they work to put into operation the constitutions of their dreams. Guideposts of minimum standards, affected by international norms and HR standards.[49] In this regard, legal pluralism, normative impacts of HR, and its standard settings are considerable.

After decades of ups and downs progress in building the rule of law in suffered societies from malfunctioning legal systems, i.e., constitutions, the development community has turned its attention to legal pluralism. Legal pluralism got the attention as a prominent feature in many development contexts for the rule of law. The questions revolve around whether alternative legal forms in legal pluralism situations might satisfy the rule of law functions that failing states cannot provide.[50] The understanding of the rule of law typically applied to state law, though sometimes to IL.

---

[48]John Martin Gillroy, *An evolutionary paradigm for international law: philosophical method, David Hume, and the essence of sovereignty*, First edition. ed., Philosophy, public policy, and transnational law (New York, NY: Palgrave Macmillan, 2013). Cover image http://www.netread.com/jcusers2/bk1388/626/9781137376626/image/lgcover.9781137376626.jpg. P108.

[49]Katharine G. Young, *Constituting Economic and Social Rights*, ed. Martin Loughlin, John P. McCormick, and Neil Walker, Oxford Constitutional Theory (Great Britain: Oxford University Press, 2012). P12.

[50]Brian Z. Tamanaha, "The Rule of Law and Legal Pluralism in Development," *Hague Journal on the Rule of Law* 3, no. 1 (2011), https://doi.org/doi:10.1017/S1876404511100019.

A familiar form of legal pluralism involves norms and institutions identified with custom, tradition, or religion or informal or village tribunals, operating alongside state legal institutions. Accessible knowledge legal varieties experienced in pluralism and fusionism put constitutional orders under the strain of updates and use of other ways of functions, especially on failed legal systems.

1.4 Comparative Analysis in Transnational Perspective

The term transnational designates untraditional types of international and national collaboration among both public and private subjects. Its concept multidimensionally links economic, scientific, and technological spheres with political and legal processes. Transnational provides features neither public nor private nor purely international, supranational nor denationalized.[51]

The conceptual frame intends to be universally appropriate and compatible with different constitutions. Using this deep thought of IL, do not provide a single overarching index with a single score for each constitution. This approach modifies the current HR and IL Indices from several other aspects and methodologies and offers an abstract form of measurement, allowing policymakers and practitioners to use the Indices to inform policy decisions on political and social developments by analyzing global and regional constitutional trends.

The primary approach is to compare the constitutions with IL and HR and evaluate them among themselves by indexes. I.e., drawing a setting for constitutional ranking based on Il and HR comparative analysis. Later it can be updated, comparative, regionally, religiously, qualitative, and quantitative to used numbers of HR. Notwithstanding IL, HR and CL are different, therefore looking for distinct topics, and classifying them in separate spheres, needs a fertile (hub) to connect here called ***transnational***. There is a need for an artful comprehensive interdisciplinary comparative method that can apply simultaneously to them and can render results in an understandable image. Hence some systematic empirical framework is needed.

While IL studies and governs external, bilateral, and orders of states (peripheral) HR tries to provide rules and bases of rights for humans from out to in which should be applied by states and CL as a catalyzer organizes relations of human and states and external organs.

CL studies and governs the internal issues of states and relations between the official authorities and individuals as well as the relations between individuals themselves. Rights are the foundations that connect these two legal branches in multidimensional and multilevel aspects that transnational names (Fig. 1.4).[52]

---

[51] Christian Joerges, Inger-Johanne Sand, and Gunther Teubner, *Transnational Governance and Constitutionalism*, International Studies in the Theory of Private Law (US and Canada: Hart Publishing, 2004). P2.

[52] "The Relationship between Public International Law and National Law," accessed 08 March, 2016, https://sites.google.com/site/walidabdulrahim/home/my-studies-in-english/state-responsibility.

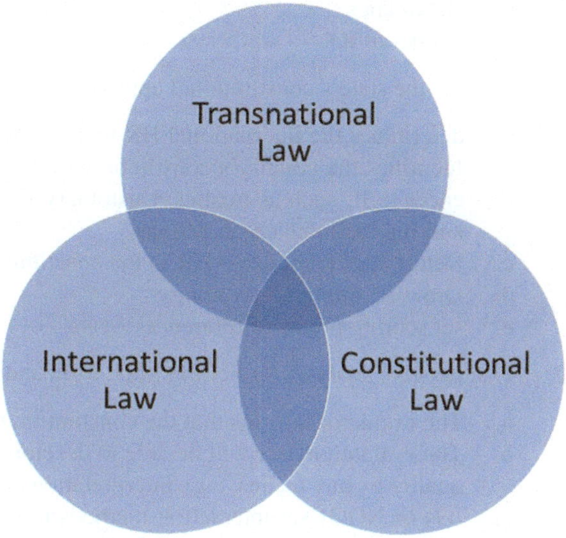

Fig. 1.4 Transnational connections dimension

1.4.1 The Evaluation Methodology

In a precise determination of IL and HR merit, worth, and significance, in constitutions by a set of standards. The result can scholarly assist any intervention or initiative to assess stated aim, realizable concept/proposal, or any alternative to help IL, HR seekers, and constitution-makers; It may be able to ascertain a theoretical rank of achievement or value concerning the aim and objectives and results of any such constitution that has been completed. In addition to gaining insight into existing initiatives, the primary purpose of evaluating a constitutional structure is to enable reflection and identify probable results.

As an argumentative practice, IL is about persuading target audiences such as courts, colleagues, politicians, and their structures and readers of legal texts about the correctness, lawfulness, interpretations, legitimacy, justice, permissibility, validity, etc. of their status. Therefore, what passes for a method, has to do with what counts as IL's persuasive arguments. Passkey of deepness is a recognizable argument as genuine legal evidence and not, e.g., a strong moral point, a plausible political position, or a convincing.[53]

The Evaluation methodology is set with three arguments along with subsidiaries. The method is multidimensional and follows:

1. Define the IL instruments for the evaluation:

    a. IL treaties.

---

[53]Martti Koskenniemi, "Methodology of International Law," in *Max Planck Encyclopedia of Public International Law [MPEPIL]* (Oxford Public International Law, 11 Dec 2014 2007). http://opil.ouplaw.com/view/10.1093/law:epil/9780199231690/law-9780199231690-e1440#.

   b. HR treaties.
   c. joinder to IO.

2. Identify the state's constitutional approaches to IL:

   a. determines the International HR treaties that the country is a member.
   b. Identifies the country's constitutional reference to IL, e.g., explicit references to IL such as treaties, Customary IL, International HR treaties, IL, and International organizations.
   c. Determines recognized HR in the constitution.
   d. Draw a compliance typology.
   e. set scoring points of references.

3. Comparative analysis for Setting Max, Min, and standards:

   a. The evaluator informs that the constitution rank refers to IL and HR.
   b. The evaluation user will be able to develop its constitutional performance quality by any means, e.g., interpretation and amendments.
   c. IOs or NGOs set interaction methods to cover their demands and goals. Methodologies of comparative CL vary in what they aim to do and their subjects of comparison, mainly in case the comparative enterprise is defined broadly to cover doctrine produced by courts, features of government, e.g., parliamentary versus presidential systems, more typically studied by governments than by CL scholars. The methodological groups have overlaps, and a single work may include examples of multiple methodologies, for instance, classificatory work and functional analysis. Simultaneously, connections of IL norms with constitutional issues raise transnational points of view for better understanding without traditional borders of International and CL. The best methodology that matches the requirements of such interdisciplinary research is comparative PL. Along with this, statistics and annalistic of common IL and HR data in a different constitution are essential. Under a PL approach to IL, parallel concepts in CL, and other international connections such as rights, PL is a foundation for all subjects to be well described and visualized in different acceptable dimensions. Comparative public (constitutional and international) law, in particular, helps part of the standard methodology of thinking about and interpreting familiar concepts from other sides.

Comparative PL here helps to reach below objects

(1) Concretize and clarify the often-common concepts IL, HR, and CL in one base;
(2) Help the balance needed for IL, HR, and CL in multidimensional visualization;
(3) Offer a uniform interpretative method for IL, HR, and CL;
(4) Ensure cross-regime consistency while mitigating the negative effects of fragmentation by stressing IL and HR commonalities with constitutional rights and openness towards others, such as transnational law;
(5) Legitimize existing jurisprudence if the solutions proposed are analogous to those of domestic courts or other international courts or tribunals;

(6) Suggest changes to legal practice given different, or more nuanced, solutions in public law.[54]

To evaluate something is to ascribe value or worth to it; then, of there being some primary category of value, e.g., the property of being right, those premises which ascribe value or worth to something in a fundamental sense of accounting is what shall refer directly evaluative premises. Directly evaluative hypotheses might describe as those who are of the form, or which entail propositions which are of the form, something is right. Legal directly evaluative propositions concerning include: the rule of law is right; i.e., there is a general moral obligation that rule of law is right; the rule of law undoubtedly possesses legitimate moral authority over its subjects, and the rule of law is appropriately justified.

Negative evaluations are not in any detail regarding this formal definition. However, premises that are of the form, or which entail premises of the form something is wrong, are also directly evaluative premises mentioned during the following dissertation.[55]

1.4.2 Comparison, Analysis, and Statistics

Comparative constitutional scholars include several broad classes of methodological approach, which may describe:

> "(1) classificatory, (2) historical, (3) normative, (4) functional, and (5) contextual, each may overlap with others in scholarly practice."[56]

For this thesis's aim, with regards to IL's HR approach, a normative methodological approach is preferred, which contributes to efforts at classification and a better understanding of the possible classification of constitutional rights on a hand and normative comparison to IL HR on the other hand.

For classification and then evaluation of constitution, after use of all comparative PL foundations, the extract data are somehow statistics, e.g., the number of rights in a constitution or articles contain IL references, analyzation and looking for their impacts or demands in constitutions before and after revolutions is the other method needed to apply such an evaluation. I.e., Comprehending when and where, even without who was writing the constitution, allows reasonable rigid predictions regarding its content. In distinct, it is predictable that the presence of a given CR with a decent deal of correctness in using expressly four factors:

(1) if any of the provided CR infringed the country's first constitution,

---

[54]"Comparative Public Law Methodology in International Investment Law," Blog of the European Journal of International Law, 2014 accessed October 17, 2015, https://www.ejiltalk.org/comparative-public-law-methodology-in-international-investment-law/.

[55]Julie Dickson and John Gardner, *Evaluation and legal theory*, Legal theory today (Oxford; Portland, Or.: Hart Pub., 2001). P51–52.

[56]Rosenfeld and Sajó, *The Oxford Handbook of Comparative Constitutional Law*. P63.

(2) the date of promulgation of the constitution,
(3) the recognized international location of the constitution provided, moreover,
(4) the enforcement percent of the constitutions in that countries' region, which infringes a given CR. On average, this pattern enables the prediction of the status of CR with 84% certainty. In other words, for the average state, it can predict precisely the infringement on 100 of the 116 rights when the only given information is the location and date of that formulation of that constitution.[57]

1.4.3 Ambivalent Approaches of International and Constitutional Law

IL and CL, both as PL branches, which exist in the same space and their subjects, are states that had influenced the other one, IL does have a considerable influence on constitutions, and several central characters of constitutions are influenced by it. Both systems' advances on a constant dialogue between constitutional orders and IL called the internationalization of CL and the constitutionalization of IL.[58]

In contemporary practice, constitutional systems usually originate with bold acts of purposive institutional design, embodied in a founding document for the polity, which involves borrowing, learning, and accommodation plus moments of creative innovation and experimentation. Any state has its type of constitution, generally sets out the framework of sovereignty power, entities and specific provisions providing HR, FR and government form way of running, which shows several legal rules and principles; In comparative view, all have many commons of IL dealing with the rule of law principles and HR, which might show, profound sameness concepts.

Gathering together disparate elements from the real or mythical national past, and the varied experience of other policies, constitution-makers produce a document to structure government and express fundamental values. Viewed in this light, founders attempt to regulate future human conduct based on speculative predictions of how institutions, sometimes untried, will function amid heated political conflicts that render compromise inevitable.[59]

More than half of national constitutions currently in force passed after the year 1990, and a third after the year 2000,[60] which are facing state obligations through IL, especially the HR realm.

---

[57] James Melton, Zachary Elkins, and Tom Ginsburg, "Whither Scotland? An Evaluation of a Proposed Constitutional Plan" (Towards a Written Scottish Constitution, Paris, France, 2013).

[58] Rainer Grote and Tilmann Röder, *Constitutionalism in Islamic Countries Between Upheaval and Continuity* (New York: Oxford University Press 2012). P77.

[59] Tom Ginsburg, *Comparative constitutional design* (New York: Cambridge University Press, 2012). P1.

[60] "Preambles of Constitutions - a comparative study of 194 current constitutions," Constitution – Making and Constitutional Change, 2015, accessed 27 Mar, 2016, http://constitutional-change.com/preambles-of-constitutions-a-comparative-study-of-194-current-constitutions/.

Twenty-four new constitutions in less than 20 years, and lots of amendments have been made regarding the HR tendency and the will of people.

(1) 2015: Yemen (interim), Dominican Republic, Congo, Central African Rep., Nepal;
(2) 2014: Egypt, Tunisia, Thailand (Interim);
(3) 2013: Zimbabwe, Fiji;
(4) 2012: Syria, Somalia;
(5) 2011: Libya (Interim), South Sudan (Interim);
(6) 2010: Kenya, Guinea, Madagascar, Niger.

Afghanistan (2004), Iraq (2005), Swaziland (2005), Bhutan (2008), East Timor (2002), Myanmar (2008).[61] Series of constitutional upgrades and their tendencies for compatibility to modern and IL and HR shows an expectation based on increasing constitutional quality beyond the state contexts.

[61] "The Endurance of National Constitutions," Cambridge University Press, 2009, accessed 24 Mar, 2016, http://comparativeconstitutionsproject.org/chronology/.

Chapter 2
Indexation of National Constitutions via International Law

Abstract How to classify national constitutions through international law? This chapter provides a theoretical method to classify the national constitution using International law and human rights normative approaches. In drew framework, primarily, there are classifications based on international law and human rights factors. i.e., classify a group of row constitutions based on their approach to international law and then human rights. Furthermore, the classification of a group of regional constitutions is based on their regional HR instruments' approach. At last, the classification is based on the number of rights mentioned in constitutions concerning international instruments. Through these classifications, three groups of constitutions are presumed:

(A) constitutions with reference to international law/international human rights.
(B) constitutions without references to international law/international human rights.
(C) constitutions with reference to regional/religious instruments regarding human rights.
(D) constitutions without references to regional/religious instruments regarding human rights.

2.1 International Law Classification of Constitution

Classification of constitutions referring to the IL. E.g., traditional dualist and monist do not suit modern needs and comparative and evaluative approach to constitutions. Following traditional classification lacks many sorts of generally recognized concepts of constitutions growing in references and multilateral use among states, international conventions, and HR treaties. There needs a modern one that is more compatible with the evaluation hypothesis. However, traditional classification can have value as the foundation of the modern one. What here called the modern classification is updated useful references in constitutions related and connected to IL. Establishing a modern classification requires first a reference to traditional, here foundations are provided, and then the modern classification based on that is provided too.

A. Shirvani, *Transnational Evaluation of Constitutions*, SpringerBriefs in Law,
https://doi.org/10.1007/978-981-16-2976-1_2

2.1.1 *Traditional Classification*

There are two major theories on the relationship between Public IL and national law (here can reference constitutions). The first is the dualist theory. The second is the monist theory.[1]

2.1.1.1 Dualist

Considers that IL and NL are two separate legal systems that exist independently of each other. Each of them regulates different subjects, functions on different levels, and each is dominant in its sphere. Public IL primarily regulates the conduct of sovereign States, and NL regulates the conduct of persons within a sovereign State. Neither legal system directly has the power to shape or modify the rules of the other. When NL provides that IL be applied in whole or in part within its jurisdiction, this is an exercise of NL's authority in adopting or transforming IL's rules into its legal system, and NL keeps supremacy. In any case of conflicts between these two legal systems, a national court would apply NL.

The dualists regard NL can apply IL only when it has been fused into municipal law. Fusion can result from an act of parliament or other political act or given effect by the courts. United Kingdom's legal system is a dualist sample. A treaty does not affect English domestic law unless it is made part of it. Once a treaty is fused into British Law, it is fully enforceable, and courts can apply it to the cases. Although the fact that a treaty is part of the national Law not necessarily mean individuals have a cause of action arising from that treaty. The fusion of the treaty changes domestic law or requires the raising of revenue or alteration of taxation. As in many international instruments in foreign relations, ratification is a formality, and fusion is not needed. An unfused treaty has no formal standing in such a system of law. If it conflicts with a statute or common law, the latter will prevail. A ratified treaty turns to a part of the land's law, but it has no particular position. The relationship between the ratified instrument and other legislation is the same as the relationship of two statutes to each other. Parliament is highest in the function "that it can pass legislation that is inconsistent with any international treaty obligations, which, nevertheless, binds the United Kingdom at the international level."[2]

2.1.1.2 Monoist

Upholds the unity of all law, regards IL and NL as setting part of the same legal system. It holds that both laws are at the same level, that of regulating the conduct and the welfare of individuals. However, it asserts the supremacy of IL over NL even

[1]Abdulrahim, "The Relationship between Public International Law and National Law."

[2]"Compilation of International Norms and Standards Relating to Disability," United Nations, accessed 11 Mar., 2016, http://www.un.org/esa/socdev/enable/discom101.htm#15.

within the national sphere; in a conflict between the two laws, IL is higher. Monists regard IL and NL as parts of a single legal system, and in their view, NL is subservient to IL.

E.g., the Netherlands is a Monist legal system. There is no national order required to convert IL into IL for the operation of treaties and international organizations' orders within the legal system. IL operates automatically within the national legal system. Therefore, certain treaties are considered constitutional laws to limit or extend Dutch offices' powers based on national CL. E.g., the **European Convention for the Protection of Human Rights and Fundamental Freedoms** and the ICCPR.

As a generalization, civil law countries are more likely to be Monist, recognizing the direct effect in the domestic law of both customary IL and treaties to which the state is a party as long as the convention is defined as self-executing. There are variations between such states regarding the status accorded IL, but it is often hierarchically superior, at least to the statute.

Common law countries, by contrast, are more likely to be dualist, requiring treaties to be incorporated into domestic law by legislation even where, as is usually the case, they accept the direct effect of customary IL. An incorporating statute has the same status as other legislation, and breach attracts the same array of domestic judicial remedies. The distinction is not neat along jurisdictional lines.[3]

2.1.1.3 Other Approaches

Another approach is somehow a modification of the dualist, attempts to establish a recognized theoretical framework tied to reality. This approach begins by denying that any common field of operation exists between IL and municipal law by which one system is superior or inferior to the other. Each order is supreme in its sphere.

A question may term conflict of obligations, happens when the state does not act by its obligations within its domestic sphere as laid down by IL. In such a case, the national position is unaffected, however as the state operates internationally, it has broken a rule of IL, and there would be a remedy that lies in the international field.[4]

It may say, the position taken by each of these two theories is a reflection of its ideological background. The dualist theory adheres to positivism, while the monist theory follows natural law thinking and liberal ideas of world society. While one of the principal catalysts for convergence is the influence of IL on domestic constitutional systems, understood to include the intense impact of supra-national arrangements within Europe on the constitutions of participating states, for the moment at least, the degree of correlation between legal systems (IL and CL) and makes a valuable tool for rights comparison. Moreover, in many cases, superficial convergence

---

[3]Mark V. Tushnet, Thomas Fleiner-Gerster, and Cheryl Saunders, *Routledge handbook of constitutional law*, Routledge handbooks, (Abingdon, Oxon; New York, NY: Routledge, 2013). Table of contents only http://www.loc.gov/catdir/toc/fy14pdf01/2012027701.html. P73.

[4]Malcolm N. Shaw, *International Law* (United States of America: Cambridge University Press, 2008). P133.

masks underlying differences in how constitutional institutions and principles are understood, explained and discussed. In this view, the relevance of the distinction is unlikely ever to disappear entirely.

Moreover, this is not negative. The different ways of thinking about constitutions derived from different legal traditions enrich the constitutional commons of the twenty-first century's world.[5] This dissertation clarifies, the monist-dualist distinction has fundamental limitations to classify constitutional approaches to IL.

(a) because they derive from a theoretical debate about the nature of IL rather than an effort to classify existing legal systems, neither theory offers an adequate account of the practice of international and national courts, whose role in articulating the positions of the various legal systems is crucial.
(b) national systems do not adopt a unified approach to IL; most of them combine aspects of the monist and dualist approaches. Like the United Kingdom, treaties do not become part of domestic law unless implemented by Parliament, while courts may directly apply international custom.
(c) because the distinction is articulated at a high level of generality, scholars sometimes differ in whether a particular country should correctly be classified as a monist or a dualist.

For example, while many observers consider France to be a monist country, some scholars maintain that, because the direct effect and superiority of treaties in France do not rest on their international validity but the French constitution, the country is dualist.[6]

For such reasons, it would be better to go beyond the monist-dualist distinction to provide a more detailed picture of states' constitutional approaches to IL.

The first constitutional issue happens when IL requires a country to carry out its international obligations; in general, the processes used by a country to carry out such obligations will vary. E.g., from legislative, executive, and judicial measures, which might seem like a first constitutional matter, countries follow different practices in facing treaty norms that incorporate treaties through the country's constitutional structure so that state authorities can implement the provisions.

(1) Self-executing.
(2) Non-self-executing.
(3) Transformation.

Countries incorporate treaties and norms into their domestic laws by specific devices called transformational. A second method, particular transformation, requires legislation to give treaties domestic effect. In the absence of exclusive agreements, a country will decide how to carry out its international obligations.[7]

[5]Tushnet, Fleiner-Gerster, and Saunders, *Routledge handbook of constitutional law*. P74.

[6]Hugues and Versteeg, "International Law in National Legal Systems: An Empirical Investigation." P470.

[7]"Compilation of International Norms and Standards Relating to Disability."

2.1.2 *Modernized Classification*

Paragraph (b), (c) and (d) article 38 of the statute of International Court of Justice provides the original virgin of national laws with this regard; Through which can discover dynamic features of Westphalian concepts; Modernized classification shed lights on the covert aspects of traditional points of international and constitutional law which are demonstrated by the contest of each member of the UN in its constitution which finally enable evaluation of constitutions. Nutation between international and CL also needs vigorous reciprocal relevancy that the transnational approach and comparative view may cover. This part extracted international start connections in constitutions to provide a connected scheme of these linked areas. From the traditional Westphalian concepts to contemporary IL notions, the emergence of other dimensions of such notions justifies the need for comprehensive interdisciplinary on such issues.

Some IL sources and concepts have dimensions and intersections in comparative and transnational points of view. E.g., customary IL, as evidence of a general practice accepted as law, forms of government, or others stated in their constitutions and used by their governments for international relations, or the general sources of law recognized by civilized nations, which aver by constitutions, have such dimensions. In this regard, IL is, in fact, less fragmented than suggested by the overflowing discourse. Empirical findings on the scarcity of conflicts, the conventional scheme of parallelism and reconciliation of norms from different regimes, and the migration of norms from one regime to another suggest that fragmentation problems have been overstressed. The diversification of international legal regimes should be welcomed as manifesting a political will of law entrepreneurs and IL's capacity to address global problems.

Internal elements of sovereignties moving in the international space, constitutional structures, national legal elements, in some cases, decisions, policies, and political developments are having an increasingly wide-reaching impact. State authority and power have become diffused in the increasingly internationally characterized concepts. The freer trans-border movement of ideas, people and concepts, and objects are boosting these multidimensional moves. Some IL scholars believe that the current world order is emerging based on a complex interconnection of transnational tracks. As for the transnational legal order, there requires sufficient dialogue between constitutional bodies with more public appearances.

Nutation between international and CL also needs vigorous reciprocal relevancy that the transnational approach and comparative view may cover. This part extracted international start connections in constitutions to provide a connected scheme of these linked areas. From the traditional Westphalian concepts to contemporary IL notions, the emergence of other dimensions of such notions justifies the need for comprehensive interdisciplinary issues.

Not all but almost short named words are from the comparative constitutions project and a CCP survey instrument named Cross-National Historical Dataset of Written Constitutions; in order to use them in the purposes of this thesis and make them useable in evaluation analysis, it was necessary to change some.[8] The following categories are referring to the primary and sub questionnaires of related IL issues in the classification of the constitutions:

(1) The title of the constitution
(2) International title of the country
(3) International, descriptive title of the state/type of the system, e.g., Republic as an international common well known one
(4) IL provisions of the constitution
(5) Treaty/Convention provisions of the constitution
(6) Customary IL terms or references of a constitution
(7) Constitutional Provisions on IO
(8) Age and Endurance
(9) Model
(10) Sovereignty, people, or divine, philosophical, or ideological approach to the ruling power
(11) Foreign Investment
(12) Foreign Trade
(13) Head of Foreign Affairs.

The description of the above categories is explained below. Whether positive or negative, the answer limits to the following three types. A crucial part of either transforming constitutional concepts to international or international concepts to constitutional ones used here; Moreover, indicators have to be evaluative, and there need clear and understandable answers. The three types of answers are:

(a) open-ended responses
(b) single-answer multiple choice
(c) multiple-answer multiple choice.

All the codes used below are provided mainly by the constitution project; however, some have been modified for more adoptions.[9]

2.1.2.1 DCTTL

What is the document entitled? Constitution, 2. Fundamental Law, 3. Basic Law,[10] other, needs explanations, Undeterminable or Not Specified. E.g., **Saudi Arabia**

[8]"Cataloging the Contents of Constitutions," Comparative Constitutions Project, accessed 27 Mar., 2016, http://comparativeconstitutionsproject.org/research-design-cataloging-the-contents-of-constitutions/.

[9]Zachary Elkins, Tom Ginsburg, and James Melton, "Characteristics of National Constitutions, Version 2.0" (2016). http://comparativeconstitutionsproject.org/download-data/.

[10]Saudi Arabia 1992 (rev. 2013).

1992 (rev. 2013) basic law and the **Australian**[11] Constitution Act. The preamble of the constitution of **Turkmenistan** is the Basic Law of the state.[12]

2.1.2.2 CNTRY

Does the constitution introduce a category or face for its international name? What is the Formal name of the country written in the constitution? E.g., **Commonwealth of Australia** and the **French Republic.**[13] Does it have any adjective to the name in international use?[14] E.g., a republic in the above example. Islamic republic for the **Islamic Republic of Afghanistan,**[15] wherein Art. One of the constitution states that Afghanistan is an Islamic Republic state.

2.1.2.3 INTLW

Does the constitution refer to IL or contain provisions concerning the relationship between the constitution and IL?[16] E.g., the constitution of the **Republic of Armenia,**[17] Art. 13. states that its foreign policy is based on IL intending to establish good-neighborly and mutually-beneficial relations with all states. Another sample is the **French Republic** constitution, which states that it respects the rules of public IL.

2.1.2.4 INTRGHT

Does the constitution refer to any international HR treaties or instruments?

2.1.2.5 INTTRT

How does/Does the constitution mention international treaties?[18] Affirmative/No; different terms/Undeterminable/needs explanations. E.g., the Islamic Republic of

---

[11] 1901 (rev. 1985).

[12] Turkmenistan 2008 (rev. 2016).

[13] 1958 (rev. 2008).

[14] Which use in international affairs such as treaty ratification or UN membership, see: "Member States of the United Nations," United Nations, accessed 26 Mar., 2016, http://www.un.org/en/members/.

[15] **Afghanistan 2004.**

[16] For purposes of this question, any mention of IL is sufficient (including such formulations as general principles, treaties, custom, international obligations, norms, commitments, etc.).

[17] 1995 (rev. 2015).

[18] Some might refer to other terms like agreements rather than treaties.

Mauritania's constitution[19] proclaims in its preamble strong from spiritual values and from the radiation of civilization attached to Islam and democracy as defined by the UDHR and by the ACHPR as well as in the other international conventions. There is no rule of general IL that all treaties must affect NL or ordinary law. Many treaties do not have domestic legal outcomes and do not require implementation through their members' national legal systems. E.g., the freedom to choose different methods of application mentioned in the ICCPR. Art. 2 Where not already provided for by existing legislative or other measures, each member to the Covenant begins to take the necessary steps, under its constitutional rules and with the provisions of the Covenant, to adopt necessary legislative or measures need to give effect to the rights recognized in the Covenant.

The adoption of a treaty typically occurs by the states' consent participating in its drafting or by a majority at an international forum. A treaty only binds those states that have consented to be bound by it and for which the treaty has entered into force. There are several procedures whereby states may express their consent to be bound. Such as ratification, acceptance, approval, or accession, depending on what the treaty stipulates and on the relevant national practice. It is increasingly common for states to sign a convention first, subsequently submit it to their legislature for approval, and finally ratify it. Several years may pass from the time of adoption until the treaty is ratified.

2.1.2.6 INTRTCNT

What is the status of treaties in the two positions of first default, second vis a vis the constitution, and are they reviewable to be in accordance with the constitution? (in case affirmative answer to section 4 above); the answer mainly concerns the status of treaties on the constitution and ordinary law. It determines whether treaties are superior or inferior to the constitution or ordinary law. e.g., the status of treaties vis a vis ordinary law is equal.[20] Treaties are inferior/superior. They are left explicitly to other legislation rather than constitutionals or need explanations/not Specified. These questions are asked if applicable. E.g., any international treaty or other such instruments that are not incompatible with **Mongolia's** constitution are not enforceable.[21]

1. Treaties are incorporated, i.e., the process that makes them part of a sovereign state's municipal law. Signing, ratification, and accession are known as incorporation. Once a treaty is approved, called incorporated, E.g., Royal Decrees shall issue and amend all treaties and international agreements.[22] 2. The incorporation requires the approval of a competent body. Section 21 art. 8 of the **Republic of the Philippines** Constitution requires treaties and international agreement concurrence with a

[19] 1991 (rev. 2012).

[20] Equal means that the more recent document is superior.

[21] Mongolia 1992 (rev. 2001). Para 4 Art. 11.

[22] Saudi Arabia Basic law, art. 70.

high Senate member rate, at least two-thirds of all for validation and effectiveness.[23] The Republic of Nicaragua's constitution sets functions of its National Assembly regarding international treaties to approve or reject international instruments without the possibility to make amendments or additions to their text. International instruments may only be presented, discussed, approved, or rejected in total. The legislative approval shall give legal effect to them, inside and outside Nicaragua.[24] 3. Left explicitly to non-CL. E.g., in the **Republic of Tunisia**, laws relating to the organizing, the ratification of treaties are deemed ordinary laws.[25]

In the status of treaty vis a vis the constitution, 1. Treaties are inferior, e.g., the draft constitution of **Libya** 2016 considers ratified international treaties and conventions superior to the law and inferior to the constitution. 2. Treaties are superior. E.g., the **Republic of Tunisia** art. twenty of the constitution gives approved and ratified international agreements a status of inferior to the constitution and superior to the ordinary of laws. 3. Left explicitly to non-CL, 4. Other, need specifications, 5. Undeterminable, 6. Not Defined, 7. Nonapplicable.[26]

Here are some more examples, Art. 9 of the constitution of **Ukraine** conditions that only following introducing relevant amendments to the constitution is it possible to conclude international treaties that contravene the constitution /.../. According to art. 95.1 of the Kingdom of Spain's constitution, if a treaty contradicts the constitution, it requires an amendment; otherwise, that treaty will not pass ratification. The constitution of **Oman** prohibits authorities from issuing regulations, by-laws, decisions, or directives that contradict the provisions of international treaties and agreements which are part of the Law of the Country.[27]

Treaty/constitution also follows the inquiry, which constitutional body has the power to initiates/approve/revoke treaties? Each part of the question may be answered by below:

1. Head of State[28] HDS
2. Head of Government HDG
3. The Government/Cabinet GVN/CBNT
4. First (or only) Chamber of the Legislature FCHMB
5. Second Chamber of the Legislature SCHMB
6. Both chambers of the Legislature are required BCHMB
7. Left explicitly to non-CL LCL
8. Other, need explanations NEXPLN
9. Unascertained or not specified NSPCFD

[23] Philippines 1987.

[24] Nicaragua 1987 (rev. 2014). Art. 138.12.

[25] Tunisia 2014, art. 65.

[26] One should not simply imply inferior status if treaties are reviewable for constitutionality; it is looking for a more explicit statement. On the other hand, if treaties contrary to the constitution cannot be concluded, or the constitution must be modified before such treaties are ratified, treaties should be coded as inferior to the constitution.

[27] Oman 1996 (rev. 2011). Art. 80.

[28] Use this choice for single executive systems.

10. Undeterminable UDTRMNBL.

2.1.2.7 INTORGS

Is there any provision related to the IOs, in case affirmative, how? Different terms/Undeterminable. E.g., Specific powers of the **Czech Republic** authorities may be transferred by treaty to an IO.[29]

2.1.2.8 CSTINTLW

Does the constitution refer to the law of nations or customary IL? Affirmative/No; Undeterminable. In case affirmative, what is the status of customary IL in the constitution? 1. Directly binding, 2. Directly binding and superior to ordinary law, 3. Requires incorporation, other, Unable to Determine, Not Specified, Not Applicable.

The generally recognized IL rules are regarded as integral parts of Federal law in the **Republic of Austria's** constitution.[30] The Supreme Court of Justice of the **Oriental Republic of Uruguay** shall try all offenses against the law of nations; questions relating to treaties, pacts, and conventions; and take cognizance of cases involving diplomatic representatives such cases as are contemplated in IL.[31] The constitutions of **Sri Lanka** and **India** refer to offenses committed on land or the high seas or in the air against the law of nations.[32]

2.1.2.9 ENDRNC

When was the latest promulgation of the newly written/amendment/reinstated constitution, or formally adopted and put into force? This question considers the importance of vernacularization to check how the old conventions and terms affected the constitution. In case a constitution has been updated after accession to a convention, is there any effect of related provisions on the constitution, particularly HR conventions.

SVRNGT

How does the constitution introduce the sovereignty of the people of the state or nation? 1. The People, 2. The State, 3. Both, 4. Neither, other, terms or Undeterminable. E.g., the people are the single origin of state power and the bearer of sovereignty in the **Republic of Belarus**. They exercise their power directly through

[29] Czech Republic 1993 (rev. 2013), Chapter 1, art. 10.1.

[30] Austria 1920 (reinst. 1945, rev. 2013), chapter 1, A, art. 9.

[31] Uruguay 1966 (reinst. 1985, rev. 2004), chapter 3 Art. 239.

[32] Sri Lanka 1978 (rev. 2015) and India 1949 (rev. 2016).

representative and constitutional bodies.[33] This term refers to the origins of rights and consequently HR of the people.

MDL

Is there any identification of a based model/ideal of the constitution? Based on which the constitution established? 1. Affirmative, examples from foreign governments/previous constitutions or state (ideologically) 3. Other terms/Undeterminable. E.g., the constitution of the **Kingdom of Bahrain** first and the second **Islamic Republic of Iran**. First, amendments base the political system of Bahrain on a constitutional monarchy with counsel shura that Islam has the highest model for governance.[34] Second, the nation intends to establish an ideal and model society by Islamic norms. Therefore, the constitution's mission is to realize the movement's ideological objectives and create promoting conditions for man's evolution by Islam's noble and universal values.[35]

FRNINVST

Does the constitution address foreign investment/foreign capital? 1. Affirmative protection of foreign investment 2. Affirmative, promotion of foreign investment 3. Affirmative, both 4. No, other terms or Undeterminable. E.g., the Federal Democratic Republic of Nepal's constitution makes the government pursue some policies, among them, policies regarding finance, industry, and commerce, providing mobility to economic development regarding industrial corridors, special economic zones, national projects, and foreign investment projects.[36] This and the below term may show the open and public international relations tied to bilateral and multilateral agreements and, therefore, probably conventions.

FRNTRD

Does the constitution mention foreign or international trade? 1. Affirmative 2. No, other terms or Undeterminable. The Republic of Korea constitution sets a constitutional commitment for the government to foster foreign trade and may regulate and coordinate it.[37]

---

[33] Belarus 1994 (rev. 2004), section 1, art. 3.

[34] Bahrain 2002 (rev. 2017), Preamble.

[35] Iran (Islamic Republic of) 1979 (rev. 1989), Preamble.

[36] Nepal 2015 (rev. 2016), part 4, 1.

[37] Korea (Republic of) 1948 (rev. 1987), art. 125.

HDFRNAFRS

Who is the representative of the state for foreign affairs? The minister of foreign affairs or answers 1–3/8–10 of the 6th question. Such information of the heads of State, Heads of Government, and Ministers for Foreign Affairs are categorized in the UN's Protocol and Liaison Service. It provides a list of all Member States based on the information provided by the Permanent Missions of each country. The changes on the Protocol and Liaison Service list.[38]

2.2 Human Rights Classification of Constitutions

Classification of constitutions referring to the HR requires multiple connection points between human and constitutional rights in international legal order and the constitutions. The core-based of this classification is first the UN charter and second, goes to the inclusive and most ratified HR treaties and then third regional and at last fourth, religious conventions, treaties or agreements.

Since its establishment, the UN has been concerned the HR and has sought to promote the right of humankind in its very founding principles, which are based on fundamental freedoms and equality of all human beings. The Charter of the UN requires member States to respect HR "for all without any distinction as to race, sex, language, or religion and forms the nucleus for the protection of rights."[39]

The supporters here are. First, the normative status of any sovereignty is finally derived from humanity, which is the legal principle that is the subject of HR. Such a normative status is also the IL's telos rather than states; second, the normative agreement among the member states, with different constitutions, very differing political, economic, cultural, and legal traditions, become necessary for an international legal framework. The increasing complexity of norms and forms of international governance and the transnational nature of many regulatory issues means that these orders inevitably come into contact with one another and, at times, with national constitutional orders.[40]

Concerning this perspective, HR is foundational in a normative sense. In this point of view, states are not ending in themselves but are composite entities whose justification lies in fulfilling public functions needed for human beings to live together in peace and security.

State sovereignty is foundational for IL only in an ontological sense because the states' mutual respect's sovereignty constitutes the "horizontal" system of juxtaposed

[38]"The Protocol and Liaison Service," UNITED NATIONS, accessed 18 October 2017, https://protocol.un.org/dgacm/pls/site.nsf/HSHGNFA.xsp.

[39]"International Norms and Standards Relating to Disability", United Nations, accessed 11 Mar., 2016, http://www.un.org/esa/socdev/enable/comp001.htm.

[40]Alec Stone Sweet, "Constitutionalism, Legal Pluralism, and International Regimes," *Indiana Journal of Global Legal Studies* 16, no. 2 (2009). P632.

actors and governs international lawmaking activity. A humanized state sovereignty implies a responsibility for protecting basic HR and the government's accountability to its people. When human needs are considered the starting point, the concentration shifts from states' rights to states' obligations vis-à-vis natural persons, and a country that does not fulfill such commitments has its sovereignty refused. The possibility of a refused state sovereignty leads, in a system of multilevel governance under the principle of solidarity, to a fallback responsibility of the international community, acting through the UNSC the ongoing process of humanizing sovereignty is the cornerstone of the current transformation of IL into a system centered on individuals.[41]

The above structure can provide legal analysis for international actors, in particular, to help states willing to bring their legal and constitutional arrangements in line with international standards and global experiences in the fields of constitutionalism, democracy, HR, and the rule of law. A modern approach identifies international standard models of constitutional rights and forms of government and different constitutional bodies. Integrates legal analysis, aiding understanding of key developments in human and constitutional rights law—Analyses HR and rights from a new perspective of transnationalism. In this regard, generally, four top classifications are available for the implementation of international HR instruments in domestic law[42]:

(1) Direct incorporation of HR identified in the international treaties into a bill of rights or constitution;
(2) Enactment of different legislative measures in ordinary laws such as the civil, criminal, and administrative laws to give effect to identified HR in the incorporated treaty;
(3) Self-executing operation of international HR instruments in the national legal order;
(4) Indirect incorporation as aids for interpreting other law. This paper is only searching for the first one.

An important aspect that distinguishes HR treaties from other international treaties relates to the duties of state parties. HR treaties are agreements between states which grant specific rights to individuals who are not themselves parties to the instruments but for whom the correlative duties fall primarily on countries. For not member states of the relevant HR treaties, generally accepted standards of HR are legally binding upon them according to customary IL.

For those countries that are not members of the relevant HR treaties, generally accepted standards of HR are legally binding upon them according to customary IL. E.g., from the perspective of NL, reliance on peremptory norms may serve as a means to try to ensure that NL does not set aside IL. In many common law countries, incorporated treaties and customary IL have a status equivalent to ordinary national legislation. Therefore, the legislature can set aside IL by enacting inconsistent domestic legislation, though the state remains responsible on the international

[41] Anne Peters, "The Merits of Global Constitutionalism," *Indiana Journal of Global Legal Studies* 16, no. 2 (2009). P398.

[42] "Compilation of International Norms and Standards Relating to Disability."

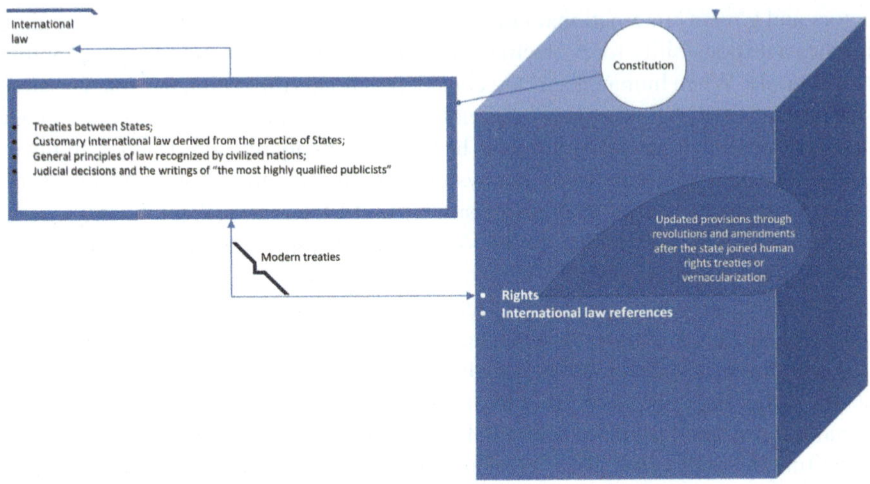

Fig. 2.1 Sources of the international law and constitutions

level by state responsibility principles. By emphasizing the comprehensive nature of a norm, litigators (particularly in the **United States of America**) have attempted to avoid these constitutional ramifications, thus far without success. A more reliable way of protecting jus cogens norms of IL within the domestic legal order would be to provide constitutional recognition of them. In the **Swiss Confederation** in the revised Swiss Federal Constitution of 1999, a new provision explicitly states that no People's Initiative (referendum) aimed at achieving a constitutional amendment may conflict with jus cogens' norms. Swiss authorities must invalidate any initiative that violates jus cogens. Such explicit recognition can serve as an emergency brake to secure respect for core international obligations at all times. The Swiss Federal Supreme Court has taken the position that in the case of conflicting obligations arising from NL and IL, respectively, the latter enjoys precedence unless the national legislature explicitly intended to adopt contradicting legislation. Therefore, this approach is similar to the one followed in many common law countries in the sense that, within the domestic legal order, the democratic will of the people supersedes IL. However, through the explicit constitutional protection of jus cogens, the international community's core values remain beyond the reach of the will of the people (unless the constitution itself is amended to reverse this position) (Fig. 2.1).[43]

[43]Dinah Shelton, *The Oxford Handbook of International Human Rights Law* (New York: Oxford University Press, 2013). P559–60.

2.2.1 Dual Sided Rights, Human, and Constitutionals

In earlier times, whenever third states openly condemned HR violations, the governments concerned countered with indicating unacceptable interference in internal affairs. Nowadays, such reasoning lost the ground when HR is at stake. The Second World War aggregated a turning point in how the international community observes its responsibility to protect and respect HR. In general, HR instruments require states to respect HR and ensure that all persons within their territory, and subject to their jurisdiction, enjoy the guaranteed rights without distinction of any kind. Although the state may derogate from some HR provisions in exceptional circumstances, such measures may, however, never be discriminatory. As time goes on, with the growth of international HR law and the repeated use of treaties to govern the treatment of nationals and while more various countries recognize due process under customary IL, rights are dual factors, constitutional and international appears more and more; and due process as a legal requirement for the states to respect all rights provided through the constitution is more common. It balances the powers and protects the person. Whenever a government harms a person without following the exact path of the law, this constitutes a due process violation, which violates the rule of law. The traditional interpretation of the principle of national sovereignty may see in two crucial and related respects:

1. How a state treats its subjects is nowadays considered a legitimate concern of the international community.
2. Such superior international standards, established by common consent, which helps evaluate ordinary laws, and the actual constitutional order, and in the exercise of their inherent jurisdiction.

Thus, whether a state has accepted international HR norms, laid down in conventions, is relevant but not the only decisive factor: HR, as formed from the UDHR, has shifted to a matter of international anxiety and does not fall within the exclusive jurisdiction of states.

The original international instrument is the UN Charter, which explicitly proclaimed HR to be a legitimate, international concern, Art. 55 provides, the UN shall promote universal respect for HR and fundamental freedoms for all humankind without distinction regarding race, sex, and other matters like religion. Art. 56 follows that all Members pledge themselves to take joint and separate action in co-operation with the organization to accomplish the purposes outlined in Art. 55.

As stated in the VDPA: "The promotion and protection of all human rights is a legitimate concern of the international community." i.e., there is a right to interfere in the case of HR violations.

Such HR interference carries the context as any form of foreign involvement in other states' affairs, which excludes involvement in coercion forms, i.e., intervention. The basis that the principle of noninterference does not apply to HR questions does not mean that states may react to HR violations by using military means but makes the distinction between interference and intervention, relevant; which is laid down in Art.

2(4) of the UN Charter, the prohibition of the use of force. Some HR experts claim that the UNSC should decide that a specific HR situation postures a threat to international peace and security, authorizing military action for humanitarian missions.

2.2.2 *Natural Rights*

The classic definition of natural rights includes the triple of life, liberty, and property; however, these need an increase somewhat, since they are not all equally basic, but form a hierarchy of derivation, with those listed later are being generally derived from those listed earlier and they are rights of personhood, rather than citizenship.[44]

2.2.3 *Limitations of Human Rights Treaties*

Like in Portugal[45] and Spain,[46] and the South African one, some constitutions explicitly provide a principle that the constitution has to interpret in conformity with international HR law.[47]

They respectively employ two distinctive types of limits on CR as inner and outer limits:

(A) Inner limits on rights concern the definitional scope of a CR and are part of the first-step process of determining whether a CR is implicated in a given situation in the first place. Thus, e.g., does the CR to liberty, autonomy, or free development of personality include the freedom to choose an abortion? Is the right to freedom of expression, including the right to expend money on political campaigns, engage in hate speech, or defame public or private individuals?

E.g., does the CR to liberty, autonomy, or free development of personality include the freedom to choose an abortion? Is the right to freedom of expression, including the right to expend money on political campaigns, engage in hate speech, or defame public or private individuals?

(B) Outer limits are constitutionally permissible restrictions on rights that are implicated and do apply in a given situation. They are part of the second-step process of specifying the circumstances in which the government can pursue a public policy objective even though they differ with and infringe a CR.

---

[44]"Classification of Rights," Constitution Society, 1996, accessed 13 Mar, 2016, http://www.constitution.org/col/class_right.htm.

[45]Portugal 1976 (rev. 2005) Art. 16(2).

[46]Spain 1978 (rev. 2011) Art. 10(2).

[47]Anne Peters, "Supremacy Lost: International Law Meets Domestic Constitutional Law," *Vienna Online Journal on International Constitutional Law* 3 (2009). P178.

E.g., where the CR to liberty, autonomy, or free development of personality is interpreted to include the right to choose abortion, the outer limit issue is when, if ever, may different public policy objectives asserted by the government limit or override that right? If the freedom of expression is interpreted to include 'hate speech,' when, if ever, may the government limit or override that right to protect its victims.[48]

IL and treaty provisions bound states in different ways. In some treaties, a member state may limit its legal obligations by reservations; a reservation renders the provision concerned non-binding or limits their effects. Parties to the treaty may also enter a declaration regarding the extent to that they wish to be bound by a particular provision or how they interpret the terms.

As most HR are not absolute, they can be limited in specific circumstances. Many HR instruments permit the restriction of some rights for reasons of national security, public order; public health; or public morality. E.g., the rights which are not absolute include freedom of movement, freedom of religion, the right to peaceful assembly, and the right to freedom of association. However, some HR instruments allow a state party unilaterally to derogate temporarily from a part of its obligations in a state of emergency.

The constitutions are the supreme law of the lands. They are the source of all political power within the nations. Every law's constitutionality and every government act is one of the most important political principles of democracies and universally the accepted rule of law norms. As a result, including the HR within the constitution seems to be the most effective way to protect them.[49]

Nonetheless, not all updated constitutions having HR brought precisely in, but rights called constitutional ones. An individual, by being able to claim the protection of a constitutional right, has what is practical, if not necessarily for philosophical purposes, the dominant general conception of a constitutional right among contemporary constitutional systems around the world, which is most essential prima facie legal claim against government infringement that can, nonetheless, be limited by specific conflicting of public policy objectives. Within this general conception, the presumption's weight in favor of the constitutional rights claims varies from one country to another and from right to right.

In chapter two, part three, the traditional classification of Karel Vasak into three generations has been discussed that it follows the principles of Liberté, Égalité, and Fraternité of the French Revolution, which is more generally on the historical development of HR. This classification, although valid for constitutional use, not complete. This classification is inconsistent with the principles of universality, indivisibility, and interdependence of HR, and the concept of generations is against that all rights are indivisible, interdependent, and interrelated.

---

48 Tom Ginsburg and Rosalind Dixon, *Comparative Constitutional Law*, ed. Francesco Parisi and Tom Ginsburg, Research Handbooks in Comparative Law, (UK and USA: Edward Elgar Pub, 2011). P388.

49 Vittoria Barsotti et al., *Italian constitutional justice in global context* (Oxford UK; New York, NY: Oxford University Press, 2016). P231.

The European Community's Human rights handbook classifies HR into two categories: first, Classic rights, and second, Social rights. The first one includes civil and political rights, which generally define the state's power in admiration of actions affecting the individual. The second includes cultural and economic rights, which require the state to act in a positive, interventionist practice to perform the necessary conditions for human development.[50] The general conception of a constitutional right is typically operationalized through a two-level process.

2.2.4 *Constitutions and Rule of Law*

The rule of law constructs the cornerstone of the theory of HR and democracy. Nonetheless, no international consensus on its meaning exists, and even in official documents, the concept is not always defined. E.g., the principle of the rule of law in the preamble to the Charter of the UN. To save succeeding generations from the infliction of war, reaffirm faith in fundamental HR in the equal rights of the people and nations, and establish conditions that justice and respect for the obligations arising from IL are supported.

In another example, The International Commission of Jurists proposed, the rule of law is more than the formal use of legal means; it is also the Rule of Justice and Protection for the members of the society against excessive governmental power. The rule of law indicates that rights have to be protected by law, separately from the ruler's will. Individual rights are to be protected against any manifestation of arbitrary power by public authorities, as well as freedoms. In sum, the rule of law means that law shall condition a government's exercise of power and that subjects or citizens will not be revealed to their leaders' arbitrary will.[51]

The first level determines whether a constitutional right is implicated and, that is, whether the prima facie claim has been established. The second step determines whether the infringement is nonetheless a justified one; that is, whether the government has rebutted this prima facie case by satisfying the constitutional criteria for limiting or overriding the right. This first step concerns the definition and scopes of the interpretation of a constitutional right; by contrast, the second involves considering the government's different public policy objectives' strength and relevance.[52]

---

[50] John C Mubangizi, "Towards a new approach to the classification of human rights with specific reference to the African context," *AFRICAN HUMAN RIGHTS LAW JOURNAL* 4, no. 1 (2004), http://www.ahrlj.up.ac.za/mubangizi-j-c#_ftnref5. P95.

[51] "General Principles Relevant to International Law," Icelandic Human Rights Center, accessed 25 Mar., 2016, http://www.humanrights.is/en/human-rights-education-project/human-rights-concepts-ideas-and-fora/part-i-the-concept-of-human-rights/general-principles-relevant-to-international-law.

[52] Ginsburg and Dixon, *Comparative Constitutional Law*. P387.

2.2.5 Flexible Integration

The constitutionalist reading of IL contributes new arguments to an old controversy that has recently emerged again, namely, the controversy over whether IL is real "law." IL's new deniers justify IL's ostensibly non-legal character by turning to the lack of complex enforcement mechanisms and the democratic deficit prevalent in IL.

The constitutionalist approach helps to overcome the narrow focus on sanctions and top-down enforcement. In most countries, CL is not enforceable. Typically, many constitutional provisions are not justiciable in the sense of being directly applicable by courts, especially in states that do not have a constitutional court but are generally valid for constitutional provisions with a programmatic, hortatory character. Despite this feature, nobody denies the character of CL as law for this reason alone. This observation supports the view that IL, resembling CL, in this respect, is indeed the law. Furthermore, the interpretation of particular norms and structures as constitutional may provide an interpretative guideline.

For example, a constitutionalist approach to reservations in HR treaties leads to permitting such reservations. To give another example, a constitutionalist-minded international lawyer will determine IL's supremacy over domestic constitutional law in a non-formalist way.

According to their substantive weight and significance, the ranking of the norms at stake must be assessed more subtly from a constitutionalist perspective. Such a non-formalist, substance-oriented perspective suggests that provisions in state constitutions with minor significance would have to give way to important international norms. Such a flexible approach appears to better correspond better to the current state of global legal integration than the idea of a strict hierarchy, particularly in HR matters.[53]

Interpreting any constitution, not those of other nations, maybe relevant political and structural differences between systems. However, constitutional experience may nonetheless cast an empirical light on the consequences of different solutions to common legal problems.

The use of outside sovereignty law in national courts raises compelling inquiries of positive theory—particularly about the relationship between different uses of other laws than nationals, i.e., "foreign law and the cross-border migration of legal norms that so far are unexplored."[54]

Similar matters have been internalized quickly by several judiciaries, with both national high courts and supranational courts participating substantially in a collaborative community of discourse about norms and principles of CL. Some scholars

[53]Peters, "The Merits of Global Constitutionalism." P406.

[54]Donald W. Jackson, Michael C. Tolley, and Mary L. Volcansek, *Globalizing Justice Critical Perspectives on Transnational Law and the Cross*, vol. Suny Series in the Foundations of the Democratic State) (United States: State University of New York Press, Albany, 2010). P 46.

have put it, the cosmopolitan turn in constitutional sources is a documented world-wide phenomenon, and judicial openness to looking beyond national borders and using comparative law arguments has become inevitable.[55]

The expansion of HR differs from the legal transplants in the international community.

(A) Despite vast differences in resources and power, HR documents come from transnational and relatively consensual deliberations, not from prototypes developed in a single colonial state. The creation of HR is now a global process, not an exclusively Western one. Insignificant ways, it is under the control of transnational elites from around the world, albeit primarily English-speaking ones. Most importantly, at least in some settings, countries participate as equals. On the floor of the UNGA, each country has one vote.

(B) HR is being appropriated worldwide by national and local actors who see the potential benefits of an HR framework and redefine their agendas in these terms. This framework provides an international audience for local problems. Thought of as HR violations, local problems become issues that a global audience can understand.

(C) HR law is far from being a consistent and coercive system of law. Preferably, it is a fragmentary and largely persuasive mechanism very much in the making. It exists in constant negotiation with nation-state law. States may contest, ignore, or adopt features of international HR law. The focus of activists is typically the state, with the international community a source of support rather than coercion. HR law is embodied in international conventions, but these take effect only when ratified by states.[56]

2.2.6 Rights and Constitutional Rights

HR law has a dual nature; it is not merely sufficient to proclaim rights; it is also necessary to identify duty-holders and their obligations. In international HR treaties, the obligations are on the states. Freedom of expression has a counterpart in the state obligation to respect the right and ensure that the individual can somehow exercise the guarantees that such right proclaims. In this formulation, the scope of state obligations is substantively both negative and positive; it is imposing a state duty to abstain from interfering with the exercise of the right. Therefore, positive obligations are generally considered to be obligations that require member states to take action. It is imposing a duty upon states to take affirmative steps for ensuring the rights protections. Negative obligations, however, permanently require states not to interfere with exercising the rights.[57]

---

[55] Barsotti et al., *Italian constitutional justice in global context*. P231.

[56] Sally Engle Merry, *Human Rights and Gender Violence Translating International Law into Local Justice*, Chicago Series in Law and Society, (Chicago: The University of Chicago Press, 2005). P226.

[57] Shelton, *The Oxford Handbook of International Human Rights Law*. P562.

All CR are rights, but not all rights are CR. In this regard, three concepts have to be distinguished:

(a) Formal

A formal concept of CR is employed if fundamental rights are defined as rights contained in a constitution, or a particular part of it, for instance, in a catalog of constitutional rights, or as rights endowed by the constitution with special protection like a constitutional complaint brought before a constitutional court.

(b) Procedural

The procedural concept of CR focuses on the institutional problems connected with CR. Recording CR in a constitution and granting a court the power of judicial review concerning all state authority is to limit parliament's power. In this respect, CR is an expression of distrust in the democratic process. They are, at the same time, both the basis and the boundary of democracy. Corresponding to this, the procedural concept of CR holds that constitutional rights are so crucial that the decision to protect them cannot be left to simple parliamentary majorities.

(c) Substantial concept

HR is at the core of the substantial concept of CR. CR is, as the formal and the procedural concept illustrate, positive, institutionalized rights, be positive law at the level of the constitution. However, this does not suffice to explain their nature. Positivity is but one side of CR, namely, their real or factual side. Over and above this, they also possess an ideal dimension. CR are rights that have been recorded in a constitution to transform HR into positive law—the intention, in other words, of positivizing HR. This intention is often actually or subjectively held by the constitutional drafters.

Moreover, over and above this, it is a claim necessarily raised by those who set down a CR catalog. This claim is a particular case of the claim to correctness necessarily connected with a law in general. A catalog of CR is correct if and only if it matches the requirements of HR. All catalogs of CR, therefore, can be conceived as attempts to transform HR into positive law. Generally, attempts to transform HR into positive law can be successful to a greater or lesser extent, which, the ideal dimension, plays a critical role even after the transformation into positive law and is of pivotal importance for the interpretation and application of CR. Their wording and the original concrete intent of the framers of the constitution by no means lose their importance. However, wording and concrete original intent are relativized by the ideal intent directed to the realization of HR.[58] In an ongoing book project on HR, scholars analyze a set of 117 different rights found in national constitutions.[59]

These fundamental material interests have been frequently designated as human or constitutional rights over the last century. The classical liberal criterion of statist protection of negative rights and market promotion of welfare has now been reached

[58] Rosenfeld and Sajó, *The Oxford Handbook of Comparative Constitutional Law*. P269.

[59] "Constitution Rankings," Comparative Constitutions Project, 2015, accessed 26 Mar., 2016, http://comparativeconstitutionsproject.org/ccp-rankings/.

by the legal protection of economic and social rights and the development of multiple institutional methods for their interpretation, enforcement, and measurement. Liberal markets and liberal democracies can exist with economic and social rights together.[60]

A. Natural, arising out of the state of nature:

   A.1. Life, immunity from being killed, except by due process.
   A.2. Limb, immunity from being injured, except by due process.
   A.3. Liberty, immunity from being confined or restricted in one's actions, except by due process.

B. Civil or social, arising out of the social compact. Includes all of the above and below:

   B.1. Property, title as distinct from mere possession, which has meaning only in a social context.
   B.2. The due process established the procedure by which different rights can be reconciled and reasonably impaired.

C. Constitutional or political, arising out of the national constitution, which has meaning only for a state with a government. Includes all of the above and:

   C.1. Denizenship, immunity from exile.
   C.2. Citizenship, immunity from being denied a vote or from holding office.[61]

2.2.7 Tripartite Typology

Since the early 1980s, a helpful definition of the obligations imposed by HR treaties has been defined by Henry Shue, which blurred the sharp dichotomy between economic, social, and cultural rights and civil and political rights. It provides three types of correlative obligations: 'to void depriving,' 'to protect from deprivation,' and 'to aid the deprived' for every fundamental right (civil, political, economic, social, and cultural). It is known today in more concise terms as the obligations 'to respect,' 'to protect,' and 'to fulfill.'

This analysis demonstrates that there is little difference in the nature of state obligations concerning different HR. "The three levels of obligation encompass both civil and political rights and economic, social, and cultural rights, blurring the perceived distinction between them."[62]

[60] Young, *Constituting Economic and Social Rights*. P56.

[61] Roland, "Classification of Rights."

[62] "Definitions and Classifications."

2.3 Rights Classifications of Constitutions

The hierarchy of HR-based classification of constitutions formulates through these inquiries, how many rights are provided in a constitution connected, and how are the rights provided, explicitly or conditional? More questions go deeper in level, and depth frequently provides a better analysis. E.g., the rights index indicates the number of rights found in any particular constitution. National constitutions increasingly reflect a commitment to HR. Some constitutions provide a list of rights in a separated section, generally known as a bill of rights. Some drafters of contemporary updated constitutions frequently reflect the language of international and regional HR norms in constructing the constitution's context.

The attitude of domestic constitutional actors towards IL is ambivalent and incompatible. On the one hand, a vertical and horizontal merging of fundamental/constitutional norms relating to HR, the rule of law, and democracy becomes evident. On the other hand, a clear hierarchy between IL and national CL, visualized as a pyramid of norms with IL at its apex, is not generally accepted by all players. This thesis's definitive judgment supports the normative suggestion to leave the model of a hierarchical relationship between IL and domestic CL since such a model is far away from the relevant actors' legal practice and not necessary to secure fundamental global values.

HR can be classified in different ways. However, each classification may face critics, therefore in ***this hypothesis, for a solution, going for rights in the constitutions and check their characters and approximation with the HR in the case is more practical***. **The other approach is to use any existed classification and analyze the constitutions with other cross-checks with the other classifications**. E.g., possible constitutional provisions got affected by HR, such as:

(1) Right to non-discrimination
(2) Right to equal treatment in specified spheres, e.g., employment or the court system, or in all other spheres of life
(3) Right to freedom from violence
(4) Different civil and political rights available to people, including the right to assembly, the right to worship, the right to free speech, and the right to privacy
(5) Different economic and social rights available to all people, e.g., the rights to health care, housing, and education.[63]

Below a sample, right-based classification shows the number, definition, and inquiries of rights. The classification goes through constitutions first and after classification, which will apply to some constitutions. After classification, the state incorporated HR or related treaties can be checked below, which may not be complete but exclusive in the sense of separated numbers and compatibility with constitutional ones and HR characters.

Rights inquiries are looking for the existence of a reference of such right in the constitution, the answers of the, in the first layer would be yes and gets one score or

---

[63] "Compilation of International Norms and Standards Relating to Disability."

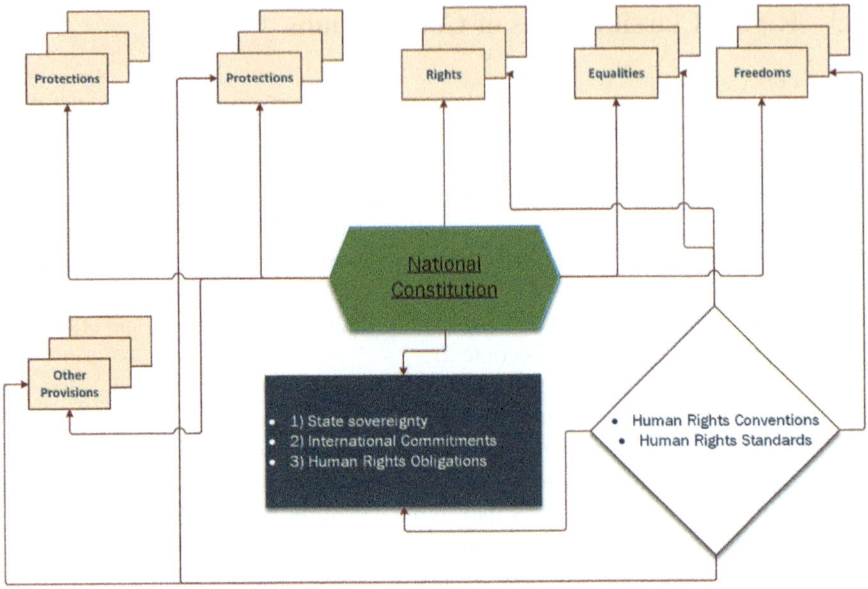

Fig. 2.2 Constitutions, international law and human rights

no without any. The inquiries can go deeper in case affirmative about if such right in the constitution is conditional or purely provided. The same as the modernized classification above in Sect. 4.2.1, the inquiries circle answers 1. Affirmative, 2. Negative, 3. Other, name in the comments section, 4. Inadequate Ascertain. If some rights are singled out for this status, please note them. In case the context defines that certain/all rights are inalienable except specified by law, it is conditional. In the following chapter, some sample constitutions will be examined through these inquiries. The full definition of the provided rights below is available at two sources or constitute and comparative constitution project.[64] However, their order and sorts have been changed to comply with this essay's purpose[65]; and some examples are provided here. Besides, whether the constitutions refer to such a right for the first level is a common question. For not making long, the definitions and questions have been omitted from 4.2.3.5 (Fig. 2.2).

2.3.1 *Rights*

One of the main similarities can be seen in the underlying rationale behind the UDHR, set out in the first recital of its preamble, namely the 'inherent dignity' and the equal

[64]"Research Design," Comparative Constitutions Project, 2016, accessed 22 March 2018, http://comparativeconstitutionsproject.org/research-design-cataloging-the-contents-of-constitutions/.
[65]"CONSTITUTE." https://www.constituteproject.org/ontology/.

and inalienable rights of all the human family; it reflects the provisions of the French Declaration, as well as the US Declaration of Independence. The thought these texts provided in the UDHR's first article also stipulates that all people are free since their birth, and second, they are equal in dignity and rights.[66]

2.3.1.1. Inalienable Rights INALRGHT

(1) Does the constitution stipulate certain rights as inalienable or inviolable?

(2) E.g., the **Andorra** constitution of 1993 not only states DGNT to be inalienable, which "guarantees the inviolable and imprescriptible rights of the individual," that constitutes the foundation of political order and justice; but also set the UDHR a binding instrument.[67]

2.3.1.2. Human Dignity DGNT

(1) Are there any references in the constitution about dignity or human dignity?

2.3.1.3. Right to Life LFE

(1) Are there any references in the constitution related to the right to life?

2.3.1.4. Right to Culture CLTRRGHT

(1) Are there any references to state duty to protect/promote culture or cultural rights?

2.3.1.5. Right to Self-determination SLFDTMNRGHT

(1) Are there any references in the constitution related to the people's right to self-determination?

2.3.1.6. Right to Equal Pay for Work RMNRRGHT

(1) Are there any references in the constitution related to the right to just remuneration, equal, or fair payment for work?

2.3.1.7. Right to Health Care HLTHCRRGHT

(1) Are there any references in the constitution to the right to health care?

(2) Are there any references to the duty of the state to provide health **care? HEALTHF**

(3) How does the constitution specify healthcare, e.g., state obligation to bear charges (free of charge)? (Fig. 2.3).

---

[66] Shelton, *The Oxford Handbook of International Human Rights Law*. P199–202.

[67] Art. 4 and 5.

2.3.1.8. **Right to Reasonable Standard of Living STANDLIV**

(1) Are there any references in the constitution related to the right to an adequate or reasonable standard of living?

2.3.1.9. **Right to Rest and Leisure LISRRGHT**

(1) Are there any references in the constitution related to the right to rest and leisure?

2.3.1.10. **Right to Strike STRIKRGHT**

(1) Are there any references in the constitution related to the right to strike?

2.3.1.11. **Right to Work WRKRGHT**

(1) Are there any references in the constitution related to the state duty for providing work/employment or the right to work?

2.3.1.12. **Right to Appeal Judicial Decisions APLJDCLDCSNRGHT**

(1) Are there any references in the constitution related to the right to appeal ordinary court decisions to a higher court?
(2) Is there any right to appeal judicial decisions for the defendant?

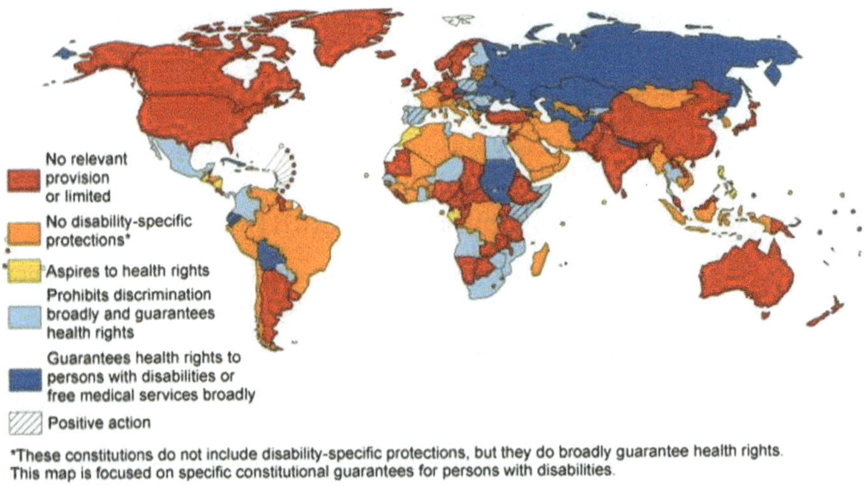

Fig. 2.3 HLTHCRRGHT for persons with disabilities in constitutions[68]

[68]"Putting fundamental rights of persons with disabilities on the map," University of California, DECEMBER 2, 2016, accessed Febuary 16 2017, https://medicalxpress.com/news/2016-12-fundamental-rights-persons-disabilities.html.

2.3.1.13. Right to Counsel CNSLRGHT

(1) Are there any references in the constitution related to the right to counsel if one is indicted or arrested?
(2) In case affirmative, how does the state provide it, e.g., at its expense?

2.3.1.14. Right to Examine Evidence/Witnesses EXMWTRGHT

(1) Are there any references in the constitution related to the right to examine evidence or confront all witnesses?

2.3.1.15. Right to Fair Trial FRTRLRGHT

(1) Are there any references in the constitution related to the right to a fair trial?

2.3.1.16. Right to Pre-trial Release PRTRLRGHT

(1) Are there any references in the constitution related to the right/possibility of pre-trial release?

2.3.1.17. Right to Public Trial PBTRLRGHT

(1) How does the constitution require trials in general, e.g., public?

2.3.1.18. Right to Speedy Trial SPDTRLRGHT

(1) Are there any references in the constitution related to the right to a speedy trial?

2.3.1.19. Jury Trials Required JRTRL

(1) Are there any references in the constitution regarding a jury or some citizen participation in rulings for criminal trials?

2.3.1.20. The trial in Native Language of Accused TRLLNG

(1) Are there any references in the constitution regarding the trial's specification in a language that the accused understands or speaks? Refers to the right to an interpreter in cases accused cannot understand the official language?

2.3.1.21. Right to Amparo AMPRRGHT

It gives citizens the right to request judicial review of government actions or judgments that they believe have violated their rights. Some legal systems (constitutions) provide a remedy or action calls the Amparo remedy r action to protect rights found in certain jurisdictions. It gives citizens the right to request judicial review of government actions or judgments that they believe have violated their rights. It is an adequate and inexpensive accouterment to protect individual rights. It is generally granted by a constitutional court and serves a dual purpose for both the citizens and the constitution itself; it ensures that any statutes do not violate its principles.

(1) Are there any references in the constitution related to the right to petition for Amparo?
(2) E.g., **the Kingdom of Spain**; Spain constitution of 1978 (rev. 2011).[69]

2.3.1.22. **Establishment of Courts of Amparo JUDCRTS3**
Establishment of courts that review government actions to determine infringements of whether related rights. Is there any specialized court to review government actions or infringements of an individual's right by the state?

2.3.1.23. **Human Rights Commission HRGHTCMSN**
An independent commission for investigation of probable violations of HR. This commission may be empowered to take action or may be required to forward its findings to the regular courts.

(1) Does the constitution institute an HR commission?
(2) E.g., the constitution of the **Republic of Azerbaijan** 1995 (rev. 2016).[70]

2.3.1.24. **Ombudsman OMBDS**
An official for investigating illegal actions of the government agencies which infringe on the rights of citizens. It enables individuals to complain about the improper actions of the government.

(1) Are there any references in the constitution related to an ombudsperson?
(2) E.g., the constitution of the People's Republic of Bangladesh 1972 (reinst. 1986, rev. 2014) (Fig. 2.4).[71]

2.3.1.25. **Right of Petition PTNRGHT**

(1) Are there any references in the constitution related to the right of the petition?

2.3.1.26. **Right to Academic Freedom ACDMCFRRGHT**
The scholars are allowed to chase their researches without the amiss intrusion of the state. It covers freedom to teach and publish too. Are there any references to any kind of academic freedom in the constitution?

2.3.1.27. **Right to Bear Arms ARMSRGHT**

(1) Are there any references in the constitution related to the right to bear arms?

---

[69] PART I, CHAPTER 4, SECTION 53, 2.
[70] THIRD PART, CHAPTER V, Art. 95I.
[71] PART V, CHAPTER I77, OMBUDSMAN.

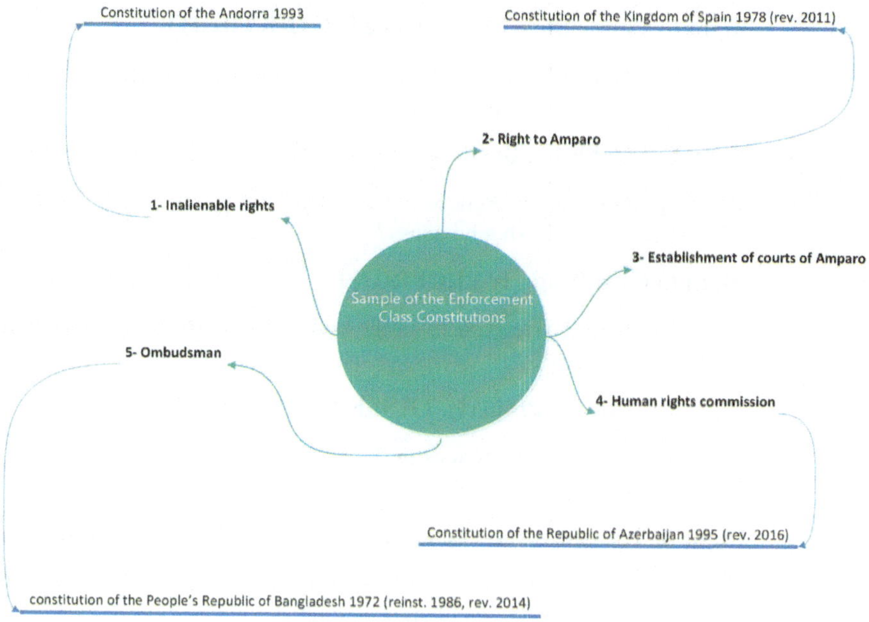

Fig. 2.4 Samples of a right-based classification (C)

2.3.1.28. **Right to conscientious objection NOMILRGHT**

(1) Is there a right for conscientious objectors to an exemption from military service, war, or other groups?

2.3.1.29. **Right to Development of Personality DVLPRSNLTRGHT**
It grants individuals the right to both develop and express their unique personalities.

(1) Are there any references in the constitution related to the individual's right to self-determination or the right to free personality development?

2.3.1.30. **Right to Marry MRGRGHT**

(1) Are there any references in the constitution related to the right to marry?

2.3.1.31. **Right to Find a Family FNDFAMRGHT**

(1) Are there any references in the constitution related to the right to found a family?

2.3.1.32. **Right to Choose Occupation OCPTNRGHT**

(1) Are there any references in the constitution related to the right to choose one's occupation?

2.3.1.33. **Right to Competitive Marketplace FRMRKTRGHT**

(1) Are there any references in the constitution related to the right to a free and/or competitive market?

2.3.1.34. **Right to Establish a Business BSNSRGHT**

(1) Are there any references in the constitution related to the right to conduct/establish a business?

2.3.1.35. **Right to Own Property PROPRGHT**

(1) Are there any references in the constitution related to the right to own property?

2.3.1.36. **Right to Transfer Property TRNSFRPRPRGHT**

(1) Are there any references in the constitution related to the right to transfer property freely?

2.3.1.37. **Right to Transfer Property Freely after Death TESTATERGHT**

(1) Are there any references in the constitution related to the right to transfer property freely after death?

2.3.1.38. **Right to Information INFRGHT**

(1) Are there any references in the constitution related to the individual right to view government files or documents under at least some conditions?

2.3.1.39. **Right to Overthrow Government OVRTHRRGHT**

(1) Does the constitution provide a right for the citizens to overthrow the government in any circumstances?

2.3.1.40. **Right to Privacy PRVCRGHT**

(1) Are there any references in the constitution related to the right to privacy?

2.3.1.41. **Right to Protect one's Reputation LIBELRGHT**

(1) Are there any references in the constitution related to the right of protection of one's reputation from libelous actions?

2.3.1.42. **Right to Renounce Citizenship CTRNCRGHT**

(1) Are there any references in the constitution related to the right of citizens to renounce their citizenship?

2.3.1.43. **Rights of Children CHLDRGHT**

(1) Are there any references in the constitution related to the rights of children?

2.3.1.44. Right to Shelter SHLTRRGHT

(1) Does the constitution provide for the right to shelter or housing?

2.3.1.45. Rights of debtors DBTRSRGHT

(1) Are there any references in the constitution related to the forbidden detention of debtors?

2.3.2 Indigenous Rights

2.3.2.1. Citizenship of indigenous groups INDCIT

(1) How is the citizenship of the indigenous groups in the constitution?

2.3.2.2. Right to Vote INDPPLGR1
2.3.2.3. Right to Representation in the Central Government INDPPLGR2
2.3.2.4. Right to Political parties INDPPLGR3
2.3.2.5. Right not to Pay Taxes INDPPLGR4
2.3.2.6. Right to Illegal Activities INDPPLGR5
2.3.2.7. Right to Self-governance INDPPLGR6

2.3.3 Freedoms

2.3.3.1. Freedom of Assembly ASSEM

(1) Are there any references in the constitution related to freedom of assembly?

2.3.3.2. Freedom of Association ASSOC

(1) Are there any references in the constitution related to freedom of association?

2.3.3.3. Freedom of Expression EXPRESS

(1) Are there any references in the constitution related to freedom of expression or speech?

2.3.3.4. Freedom of Movement FREEMOVE

(1) Are there any references in the constitution related to freedom of movement?

2.3.3.5. Freedom of Thought/Opinion/Conscience OPINION

(1) Are there any references in the constitution related to freedom of opinion, thought, and/or conscience?

2.3.3.6. **Freedom of Press EXPRESS**

(1) Are there any references in the constitution related to freedom of the press?

2.3.3.7. **Freedom of Religion FREEREL**

(1) Are there any references in the constitution related to freedom of religion?

2.3.4 Equalities

2.3.4.1. **General guarantee of equality**
It is based on the idea that every individual is equal before the law; it guarantees that they are rightful to the same privileges and immunities while prohibiting favoritism or discrimination against any group.

(1) Is there any reference to equality before the law or the equal rights of men, or non-discrimination?
(2) Which of the following matters are protected from discrimination/provide for equality in the constitution? i.e., equalities regardless of:

2.3.4.2. **Gender EQLGR1**
2.3.4.3. **Skin color EQLGR2**
2.3.4.4. **Creed or belief EQLGR3**
2.3.4.5. **Social status EQLGR4**
2.3.4.6. **Nationality EQLGR5**
2.3.4.7. **Financial status EQLGR6**
2.3.4.8. **Country of origin EQLGR7**
2.3.4.9. **Tribe or clan EQLGR8**
2.3.4.10. **Race EQLGR9**
2.3.4.11. **Language EQLGR10**
2.3.4.12. **Religion EQLGR11**
2.3.4.13. **Political party EQLGR12**
2.3.4.14. **Sexual orientation EQLGR13**
2.3.4.15. **Age EQLGR14**
2.3.4.16. **Parentage EQLGR15**
2.3.4.17. **For persons with disabilities, Mentally or Physically EQLGR16** (Fig. 2.5).

2.3.5 *Protections*

(1) Which of the following matters has got a reference for protection in the constitution?

2.3.5.1. **Expropriation EXPROP**
2.3.5.2. **Stateless person ASYLUM**
2.3.5.3. **Self-incrimination MIRANDA**
2.3.5.4. **Unjustified restraint HABCORP**
2.3.5.5. **Victim's rights VICRIGHT**
2.3.5.6. **Environment ENV**

Fig. 2.5 Number of constitutions provide equal rights for men and women[72]

[72]"Gender Equality," accessed March 18 2018, https://www.un.org/en/sections/issues-depth/gender-equality/.

2.3.6 *Other Provisions*

2.3.6.1. **Provisions for intellectual property INTPROP4**

(1) Are there any references in the constitution that mention the following intellectual property rights?

2.3.6.2. **Patents INTPROP1**
2.3.6.3. **Copyrights INTPROP2**
2.3.6.4. **Trademark INTPROP3**
2.3.6.5. **Provision for civil marriage CIVMAR**

(1) Are there any references in the constitution to the provisions for civil marriage?

2.3.6.6. **Provision for Matrimonial Equality MATEQUAL**

(1) Are there any references in the constitution related to matrimonial equality?

2.3.6.7. **Prohibition of Cruel Treatment CRUELTY**

(1) Are there any references in the constitution related to the prohibition of inhuman, cruel, or degrading treatment?

2.3.6.8. **Prohibition of Slavery SLV**

(1) Are there any references in the constitution related to the prohibition of slavery, servitude, or forced labor?

2.3.6.9. **Prohibition of Torture TRTR**

(1) Are there any references in the constitution related to the prohibition of torture?

2.3.6.10. **Restrictions on Rights of Groups**

(1) Are there any restrictions on the rights of the following groups?

2.3.6.11. **Property Owners RGHTRES1**
2.3.6.12. **Racial/Ethnic/ National Minorities /Linguistic/Religious RGHTRES2**
2.3.6.13. **Women RGHTRES3**
2.3.6.14. **Non-Property Owners RGHTRES4**
2.3.6.15. **Peasants RGHTRES5**
2.3.6.16. **Immigrants RGHTRES6**
2.3.6.17. **Elderly Individuals RGHTRES7**
2.3.6.18. **Persons with disabilities, Mentally or Physically RGHTRES8**
2.3.6.19. **Suffrage VOTERES**

(1) Can the right to vote be restricted in any way?

2.3.6.20. **Binding effect of constitutional rights BINDING**

(1) Does the constitution refer to rights provisions binding on both the private parties and the state?

2.3.6.21. **Guarantee of due process DUEPROC**

(1) Are there any references in the constitutions to the due process?

2.3.6.22. **Access to higher education ACHIGHED**

(1) Are there any references in the constitutions to equal access to higher education?

2.3.6.23. **Compulsory education EDCOMP**

(1) Are there any references in the constitutions to compulsory education until at least some level?

2.3.6.24. **Free education EDFREE**

(1) Are there any references in the constitutions to free education, at least up to some level?

2.3.6.25. **Employment of children CHILDWRK**

(1) Are there any references in the constitutions to the limits on child employment?

2.3.7 Number of Provided Rights

(1) How many of the above rights are included in the constitution?

While the number of member states to the HR treaties is increasing, HR and IL are going more and more through the states' sovereignty and obtain from them in an ambivalent approach.[73]

When the object of many HR standards is in controversy, an assertion is uncontested. Here, the law is a process and constitutes a set of rules that need to be ascertained at times and for multiple purposes. While not excluding the dynamic character of the whole phenomenon of law, this section primarily approaches IL as a set of rules that can be used to promote or protect HR. As HR standards can be found in national constitutions. The Constitutions are increasingly reflecting a commitment to such standards. At times the rights in the constitutions are listed in a section generally called the bill of rights. However, they may find in other kinds and parts too.[74]

---

[73]Joel P. Trachtman, *The Future of International Law: Global Government*, ASIL Studies in International Legal Theory, (United States of America: Cambridge University Press, 2013). P 3.

[74]Jean d'Aspremont, *Formalism and the Sources of International Law: A Theory of the Ascertainment of Legal Rules*, Oxford Monographs in International Law, (Great Britain: Oxford University Press 2011). P 1.

The number of affirmative answers to the above questionnaires that match the states' commitment to a ratified HR treaty classifies such a constitution. Here is an example, three groups provided:

(A) group A (73–107) shows the common constitutional approach to IL along with the highest number of CR in that constitution, which matches the state commitment via ratified HR treaties of the same state.
(B) Group (B 37–72) Shows the common constitutional approach of that group along with the number of the CR in that constitution that matches those state commitments via ratified HR treaties.
(C) Group (C 1–36) Shows the common constitutional approach of that group along with the number of the CR in that constitution that matches those state commitments via ratified HR treaties.

Here in visual 4 provides a sample of such classification (Fig. 2.6).

2.4 Evaluation of Constitutions and Comparative Analyzation

Many classifications help the theory of evaluating constitutions through IL; however, the best is the one with the most potential layers and depth. In the above classifications, modern on the constitution approaches to IL, the number of rights provided matches this point. The connections which go from a constitution to IL and treaties show the transnational algebraic coordinates of these concepts not precisely but approximately and dynamic. The below visual provides a dimensional view of IL and transnational law layers/depth in a PL's dimensional view.

Constitutions provide many aspects, governments, IL approaches, government structure, bill of rights, etc. Each layer has connection points in the sphere of both international and transnational law, in a more exceptional picture, PL, while the constitution itself is inside such imagination. Therefore, the decagons position here, do not mean their external subjects, but internal ones. The reason to use decagons here as the constitutions is that they provide varieties of edges needed (Fig. 2.7).

Under an evaluation, constitutions might divide into general and specialized levels. At the general level, categorization of constitutions into four ranks based on HR and the constitution approaches to IL that how it deals with IL. It suggests A, B, C, and D index for evaluation of constitutions. Rank A categorizes constitutions that have explicit references to IL and HR, B categorizes constitutions that have explicit references to HR and implicit references to IL. C, constitutions that have explicit IL references but no HR ones. Finally, D, constitutions that have neither HR nor IL references.

At a higher level, evaluation can be upgraded by analyzing the number of explicit or implicit references to rights and their category of HR categories, such as social, political, economic rights. The Dualist or monism approach is also sub-grade for A, B, C categories. Moreover, evaluation can continue in different layers of rights and

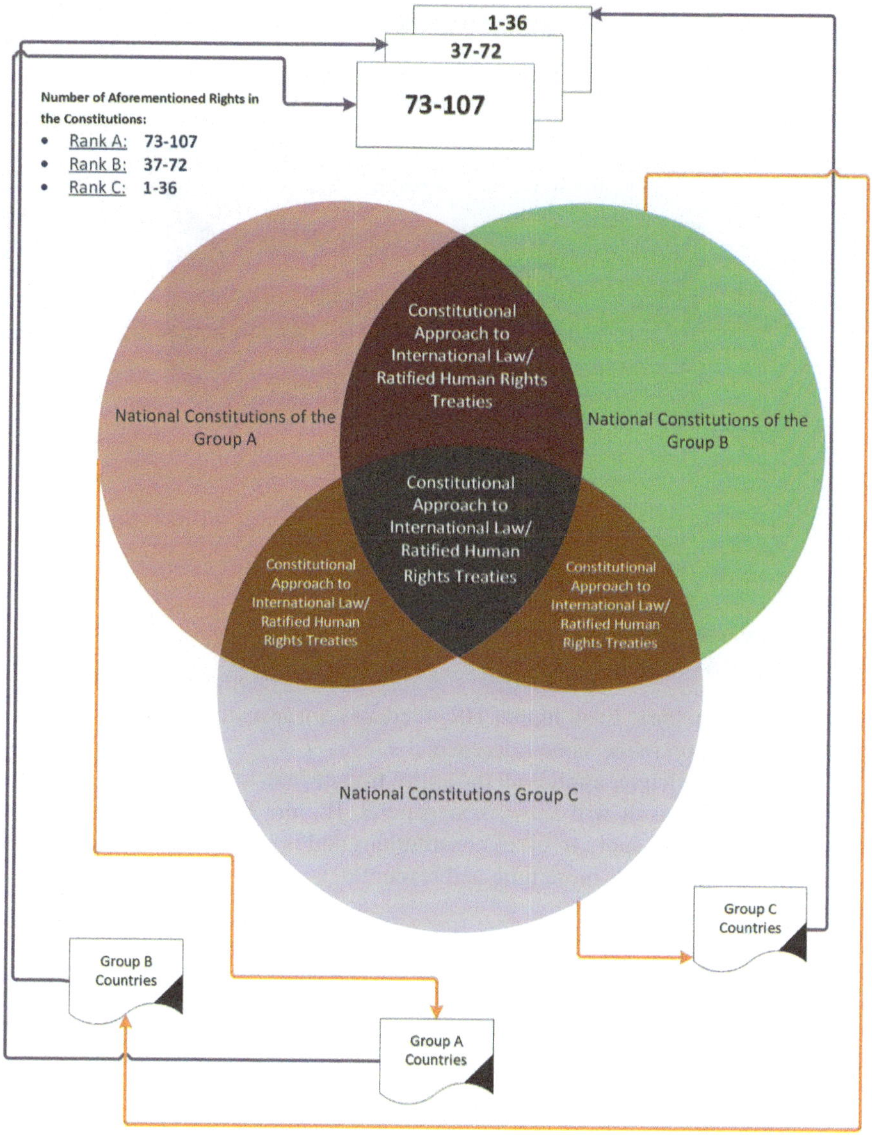

Fig. 2.6 Groups by international law and rights

IL, such as customary, self-binding rules or IL proposals of the constitution to the international community in other levels. Higher levels need a plus (+) sign for three general rankings. Specialized level scrutinizes IL and HR quantity and quality of constitutional principles if they are eventual by more laws or any superior principle. In comparison, the principles of IL reference together shape a transnational model

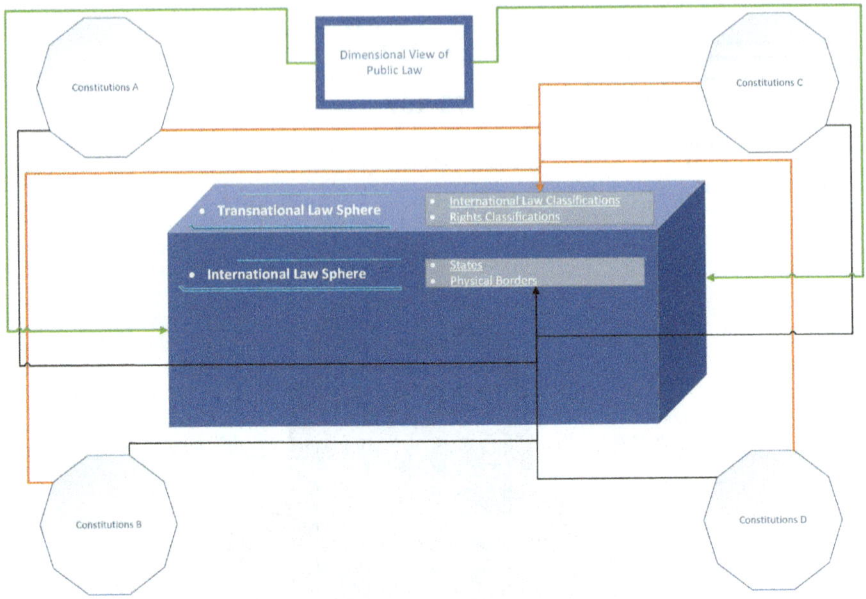

Fig. 2.7 Dimensional view of public law

of its general category. Each higher HR + creates a transnational model of such a right in comparison to the same reference.

The following chapter applies all the above frameworks to a group of four sample constitutions; the result will show their general, IL, and HR rank in comparison. This framework may apply to other constitutions and is capable of more depth and frequencies, which needs more time and resources.

Chapter 3
A Theoretical Framework for the Evaluation of Constitutions

Abstract This chapter is applying an analytical framework to evaluate four samples of constitutions through international law and human rights references of the constitutions. By this application, these constitutions will get ranks based on international law and human rights factors that analytically show their typical pattern and different results. The selected constitutions might have the most similarities in the title; however, they are separated into different continents having different social and cultural attitudes to provide how transnational concepts frame a standard model of constitutional design, here called a pattern and how might the results be the same.

The **Republic of Azerbaijan 1995 (rev. 2016)** from Asia, the **Republic of Finland 1999 (rev. 2011)** from Europe, the **Republic of South Africa 1996 (rev. 2012)** from Africa, and finally, the **Republic of Colombia 1991 (rev. 2015)** from America is the sample of this application. The most important reason for such selection is that these constitutions are young and established later than 1990, which is chronically later than most of the nine core international HR instruments. Here is the order of the main and their protocols by year, ICERD 1965, ICCPR 1966, ICESCR 1966, CEDAW 1979, CAT 1984, CRC 1989, ICMW 1990, ICCPR-OP1 1966, and ICCPR-OP2 1989.

Moreover, these four sample countries have written constitutions, and all are members of the UN and bearing international and human rights commitments through different treaties; since they are from different regions may also have regional commitments like Finland via EU and ECHR and Colombia via ACHR, which will be checked and considered in evaluation application in subsection three of this chapter (Fig. 3.1).

The other reason is that they are also common in the title of the constitutional system, Republic here. Finally, they spread on different continents, having their international title of Republic and the name of thc country. Such a title particularly and tentatively references a side of the constitutions that operate as the external face. It tags the state, identifies its people, and sets its territory from other international law subjects; inside, it structures how the state approach to international law sphere by empowering governmental institutions, limiting their authority, and defining the relations between them. The concept of a constitution is undergoing the exact effects of globalization called the Transformation of Constitutions. Below provided a visual,

A. Shirvani, *Transnational Evaluation of Constitutions*, SpringerBriefs in Law,
https://doi.org/10.1007/978-981-16-2976-1_3

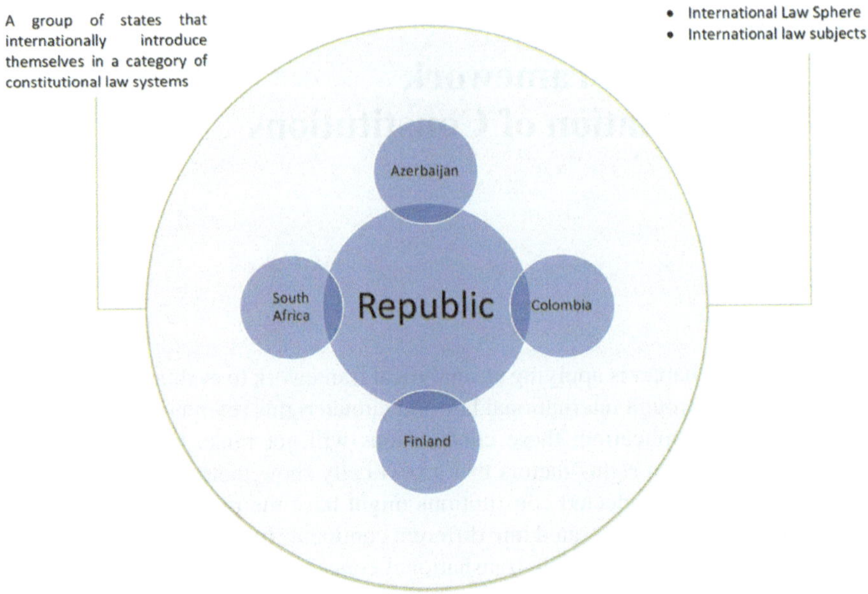

Fig. 3.1 Four samples for application of the analytical framework

tried to show that these four IL subjects, the outside face of the constitution, introduce them as a republic, i.e., their constitution is maybe not totally but mostly giving them an international title recognized officially by other states. E.g., the United Nations High Commissioner for Human Rights, called UNGEGN references to the art. 70 of the Constitution of **Switzerland 1999 (rev. 2014)** states that the Federation's official languages are German and French, Italian, and Romansh is an official language for communicating with persons in such languages. This information provided in the UNGEGN List of Country Names follows the successor to the first effort, which has been selected using Unicode-compliant fonts throughout the entries for the country members of the UN. The international community is generally recognized as independent states and countries with permanent observer status in the UN system. UNGEGN is a standing expert body of the UN Economic and Social Council (ECOSOC) and the six others.

The document's principal aim is to manifest country names in the official languages used within each country in the world. The names are provided in two forms, first the short names, which may or may not be official, and second, the formal names, which are those used in official diplomatic context resources from the constitution (Fig. 3.2).

AF	AFGHANISTAN	
Language	Short name	Formal name
National Official		
Dari	افغانستان *Afghânestân*	جمهوری اسلامی افغانستان *Jomhûrî-ye Eslâmî-ye Afghânestân*
ps: Pashto	افغانستان *Afghânistân (1)*	د افغانستان اسلامی جمهوریت *Afghânistân Islâmî Jumhûriyat (Dê)* (1)
UN Official		
English	Afghanistan	Islamic Republic of Afghanistan (the)
French	Afghanistan (l') (masc.)	République islamique d'Afghanistan (la)
Spanish	Afganistán (el)	República Islámica del Afganistán (la)
Russian	Афганистан	Исламская Республика Афганистан
Chinese	阿富汗	阿富汗伊斯兰共和国
Arabic	أفغانستان	جمهورية أفغانستان الإسلامية
Name used by a national authority		Spain: www.ign.es ("Toponimia y Nomenclátores")
Notes	(1) Romanization in the BGN/PCGN 1968 Pashto system	

CH	SWITZERLAND	
Language	Short name	Formal name
National Official		
de: German	Schweiz (die)	Schweizerische Eidgenossenschaft (die)
fr: French	Suisse (la)	Confédération suisse (la)
it: Italian	Svizzera (la)	Confederazione Svizzera (la)
rm: Romansh[1]	Svizra (la)[1]	Confederaziun Svizra (la)[1]
UN Official		
English	Switzerland	Swiss Confederation (the)
French	Suisse (la)	Confédération suisse (la)
Spanish	Suiza	Confederación Suiza (la)
Russian	Швейцария	Швейцарская Конфедерация
Chinese	瑞士	瑞士联邦
Arabic	سويسرا	الاتحاد السويسري

Fig. 3.2 UNGEGN samples of short and official names of the countries

3.1 Application of the International Law Classification

The 15 values described in chapter 4, part one, subsection two as DCTTL, CNTRY, INTLW, INTRGHT, INTTRT, INTRTCNT, INTORGS, CSTINTLW, MDL, ENDRNC, SVRNGT, FRNINVST, FRNTRD, HDFRNAFRS, and WR will be examined in the sample constitutions. The charts provided below show the values of the constitution concerning the evaluation based on IL classification. The method descriptive has also been explained below the first chart.

3.1.1 Azerbaijan

The country of Azerbaijan declared its independence on 18 October 1991, before the dissolution of the Soviet Union on 26 December 1991; it joined the UN on 2 March 1992, after the UNGA admitted Azerbaijan at its 46th session (Fig. 3.3).

3.1.1.1 Descriptive Detail of the Chart

- DCTTL, the term constitution, here repeated 166 in the constitution, and it states CNTRY as the Republic of Azerbaijan, which counts two values for both, one for each.
- Arts. One and ten explicitly refer to IL, that the Azerbaijan people obey the State and its Laws which does not exclude norms defined by the IL. The Constitution of Azerbaijan drew its relations with other States based on the principles recognized by the universally acknowledged rules of IL as INTLW.
- INTRGHT, no references, therefore the value is zero.
- The constitution refers to international treaties, INTTRT and INTRTCNT in several articles, especially 148 part 2, incorporated international treaties in the Republic of Azerbaijan are an inalienable substantive part of the legal system.

General Evaluation of the Constitution Based on International Law Values

International Name:	Azerbaijan
UNGEGN name:	The Republic of Azerbaijan/阿塞拜疆共和国
Current Constitution:	1995 (rev. 2016)

Items 1-8	Values/Comparative base	Item 9-15	Values
DCTTL	Constitution, Value=1	CSTINTLW	Yes; Art. 10, Value=1
CNTRY	The Republic of Azerbaijan, Value=1	MDL	No refrences, Value=0
INTLW	Yes; Arts. 1 & 10, Value=1	ENDRNC	2016, No, Value=0
INTRGHT	No refrences, Value=0	SVRNGT	Art.2 People, Value=1
INTTRT	Yes; several Arts., Value=1	FRNINVST	No refrences, Value=0
INTRTCNT	Art. 148, Value=1	FRNTRD	No refrences, Value=0
INTORGS	Yes; Art. 109, Value=1	HDFRNAFRS	No refrences, Value=0
TOTALS	*8 Values*		

Fig. 3.3 General evaluation of the Azerbaijan constitution based on international law

- INTORGS, Art. One hundred nine, while setting the presidential powers, refers to IO.
- CSTINTLW, Art. Ten of the constitution, refers to CIL, however not in terms but other words, that Azerbaijan foreign relations with other countries based on the principles recognized universally and acknowledged through IL.
- The constitution has no reference to any other constitution as a model, which provides zero value in this regard as MDL.
- ENDRNC, However, the latest amendment occurred in 2016, and endurance is three years since up to 2019; it does not provide any value since it is not in line with any IL or HR but constitutional matters.
- SVRNGT, Art. Two refers to the people of Azerbaijan as the sources of sovereignty and their right to freely and independently decide for their fate and establish the form of governance, which shows the human as the accel of the power rather than ideologies, e.g., religious.
- FRNINVST, no references; therefore, the value is zero.
- FRNTRD, no references; therefore, the value is zero.
- HDFRNAFRS, no references; therefore, the value is zero.

3.1.2 Finland

Finland is a modern, democratic Nordic country and a long constitutional history. The recent one goes back to the period of independence from Russia in 1917. On 4 December 1917, the Senate of Finland made a Declaration of Independence which the Finnish parliament later adopted. Despite recognition by Russia, Sweden, Norway, Denmark, Germany, France, and the United Kingdom, decided to wait and gradually, one by one, gradually recognized independence.

Finland was ineligible for charter membership in the UN in 1945. Due to its conflicts with the Axis powers during World War II, and applied for membership in 1947, which delayed the entry until 1955 refer to the Cold War disagreements among the great powers on UN admissions policies. After Finland acceded to the EU and the need to integrate and update the Finland constitutional legislation, e.g., a single constitutional act like other EU countries rather than fragmented and across several acts, lead to the process of the 1990s constitutional reform. The current constitution came into force on 1 March 2000, as an integrated constitution to replace the four existing constitutional laws in the form of a Government bill. The below charts provide a general evaluation of Finland's constitution based on IL. For more, please refer to the details of the Azerbaijan descriptive of the evaluation (Fig. 3.4).

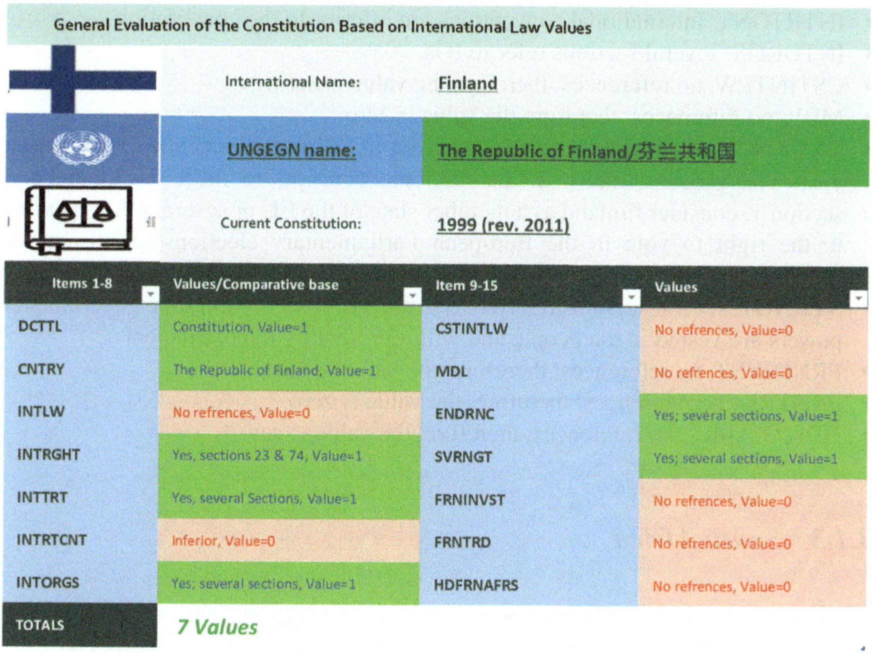

General Evaluation of the Constitution Based on International Law Values

International Name:	Finland
UNGEGN name:	The Republic of Finland/芬兰共和国
Current Constitution:	1999 (rev. 2011)

Items 1-8	Values/Comparative base	Item 9-15	Values
DCTTL	Constitution, Value=1	CSTINTLW	No refrences, Value=0
CNTRY	The Republic of Finland, Value=1	MDL	No refrences, Value=0
INTLW	No refrences, Value=0	ENDRNC	Yes; several sections, Value=1
INTRGHT	Yes, sections 23 & 74, Value=1	SVRNGT	Yes; several sections, Value=1
INTTRT	Yes, several Sections, Value=1	FRNINVST	No refrences, Value=0
INTRTCNT	Inferior, Value=0	FRNTRD	No refrences, Value=0
INTORGS	Yes; several sections, Value=1	HDFRNAFRS	No refrences, Value=0
TOTALS	7 Values		

Fig. 3.4 General evaluation of the Finland constitution based on international law

3.1.2.1 Descriptive Detail of the Chart

- DCTTL, the term constitution, repeated 59 and explicitly named the document constitution.
- CNTRY, the Republic of Finland mentioned in the first line of the constitutional text, introduces Finland as a sovereign republic.
- INTLW, no reference.
- INTRGHT, section 23, refers to provisional exceptions to fundamental rights and liberties that are compatible with the countries international HR obligations in case of an armed attack. Later section 74 states the Constitutional Law Committee considers the constitutionality of legislative proposals and matters brought for, as well as on their relation to international HR treaties.
- INTTRT, Section 94, requires accepting the parliament for treaties and international obligations that contain provisions of a legislative nature, otherwise an approval by the parliament under the constitution. The acceptance of the parliament is also required for the denouncement of international obligations. Section 95 refers to provisions of treaties and other international obligations, in so far as they have a legislative nature, are brought into force by an Act, otherwise, by a Decree. Section 97, related to providing information to the parliament on matters to be dealt with in a European Council whenever treaties establishing the EU faces any amendments.
- INTRTCNT, International conventions are inferior to the constitution.
- INTORGS, several sections refer to IOs.
- CSTINTLW, no references, therefore the value is zero.
- MDL, no references, therefore the value is zero.
- ENDRNC, the latest amendment occurred in 2011, endurance to 2019 is eight years and provided more IL and regional concepts to the constitution, e.g., section 1, consider Finland as a member state of the EU or several other sections, to the right to vote in the European Parliamentary elections, provisions on fundamental rights and liberties that are compatible with international HRs.
- SVRNGT, several sections referred to it, and section two states the governments' powers are vested in the people and will represent by the parliament.
- FRNINVST, no references; therefore, the value is zero.
- FRNTRD, no references; therefore, the value is zero.
- HDFRNAFRS, no references; therefore, the value is zero.

3.1.3 South Africa

South Africa has had four Constitutions, 1910, eight years after the end of the Second Boer War, and after an act of the British, Parliament called the South Africa Act 1909, which granted nominal independence while creating the Union of South Africa on 31 May 1910. It gave rights to the white minority but took away the right to vote for most South Africans. 1960, the white after a referendum to decide whether South Africa

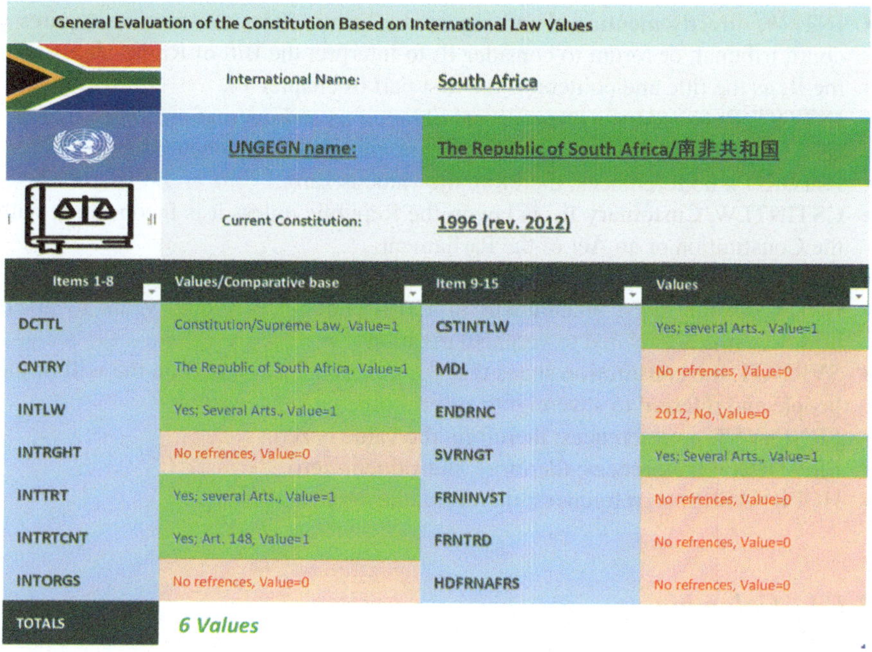

General Evaluation of the Constitution Based on International Law Values

International Name:	South Africa
UNGEGN name:	The Republic of South Africa/南非共和国
Current Constitution:	1996 (rev. 2012)

Items 1-8	Values/Comparative base	Item 9-15	Values
DCTTL	Constitution/Supreme Law, Value=1	CSTINTLW	Yes; several Arts., Value=1
CNTRY	The Republic of South Africa, Value=1	MDL	No refrences, Value=0
INTLW	Yes; Several Arts., Value=1	ENDRNC	2012, No, Value=0
INTRGHT	No refrences, Value=0	SVRNGT	Yes; Several Arts., Value=1
INTTRT	Yes; several Arts., Value=1	FRNINVST	No refrences, Value=0
INTRTCNT	Yes; Art. 148, Value=1	FRNTRD	No refrences, Value=0
INTORGS	No refrences, Value=0	HDFRNAFRS	No refrences, Value=0
TOTALS	6 Values		

Fig. 3.5 General evaluation of the South Africa constitution based on international law

would become a Republic which also took away the rights of black citizens. 1983 which created the tricameral parliament, meant to provide a separate parliament for the White, Colored, and Indian groups and excluded black people and automatically made them citizens of the homeland with no rights outside homelands. The fourth one, the 1994 constitution, was an interim one that gave the vote to everyone. The current one negotiated between May 1994 and October 1996 in a democratically elected convention for the first time. The constitution holds international experiences from other parts of the world who played a significant role in its development and in many of its provisions, which are the realization of years of internal conflicts and are imbued with historical significance (Fig. 3.5).

3.1.3.1 Descriptive Detail of the Chart

- DCTTL, While the preamble once called it supreme law, several articles called the constitution (repeated 481 times), and later directly it states that the Act called the Constitution of the Republic of South Africa, 1996.
- CNTRY, the term Republic of South Africa, repeated 116 times. The most important one, art. one introduces the sovereign, democratic state of the Republic of South Africa.

- INTLW, directly mentioned and repeated 12 times. The constitution requires a court, tribunal, or forum to consider IL to interpret the Bill of Rights. It also put the IL as the title and content of the first part of chapter 14.
- INTTRT, Referred to as international obligations and international agreements.
- INTRTCNT, International conventions are inferior to the constitution.
- INTORGS, no references, therefore the value is zero.
- CSTINTLW, Customary IL, is law in the Republic unless it is inconsistent with the Constitution or an Act of the Parliament.
- MDL, no references, therefore the value is zero.
- ENDRNC, the latest amendment in 2012, endurance is nine years to 2021; however, it is not related to vernacularization.
- SVRNGT, the constitution states that the government is based on the will of the people and referred to sovereignty several times.
- FRNINVST, no references; therefore, the value is zero.
- FRNTRD, no references; therefore, the value is zero.
- HDFRNAFRS, no references; therefore, the value is zero.

3.1.4 Colombia

The current Constitution of Colombia is the governing document since 1991; it is the ninth since 1830, which introduces the country as the Republic, which replaced the old one of 1886. Back in the nineteenth century, after an agitated constitution, in 1886, Colombia adopted its oldest constitutions which are also the oldest in Latin America. It was in force for about a century and needed some reforms to adapt to the country's changed social, economic, and political conditions. The constitution has amended several times reforms in 1993, 1995, 1996, 1997, 1999, 2000, 2001, 2002, 2003, 2004, 2005, 2015 also on 7 July 2016, 4 April 2017, 17 January 2018, however the English version available and examined is 2015 one. This constitution created mechanisms in three ways to protect certain rights:

(1) tutelage; it allows a party to bring an action to suspend any action or cancellation of a governmental or private institution that endangers a fundamental right.
(2) the Defensor del Pueblo, a Human Rights Ombudsman, elected for a four-year term by the House of Representatives, who monitors the protection and development of HR.
(3) class actions designed to protect collective interests and rights (Fig. 3.6).

3.1.4.1 Descriptive Detail of the Chart

- DCTTL, the document called the constitution in several articles, especially art. four which states, it provides the norm of regulations and put above all other statute and laws.

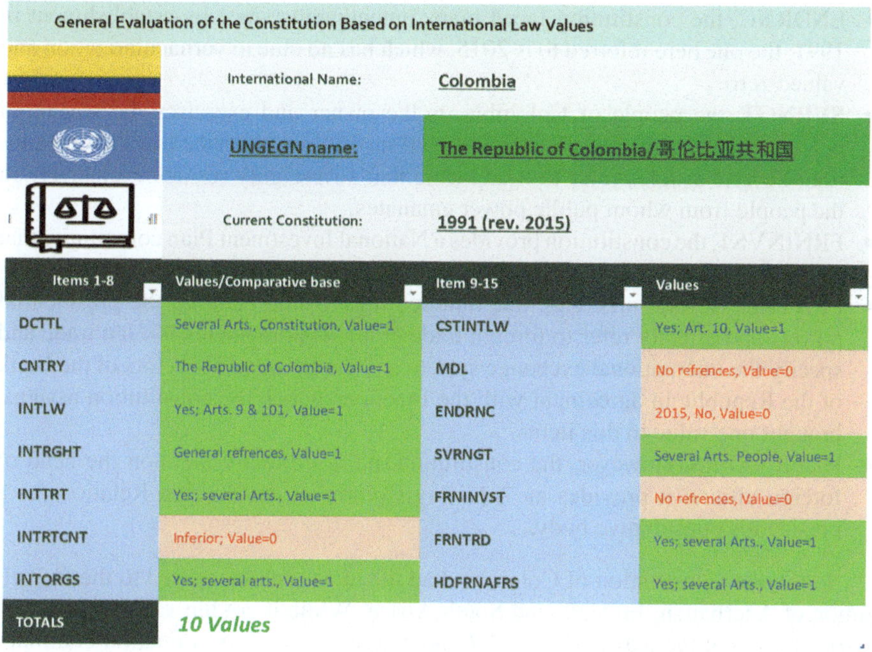

General Evaluation of the Constitution Based on International Law Values			
	International Name:	Colombia	
	UNGEGN name:	The Republic of Colombia/哥伦比亚共和国	
	Current Constitution:	1991 (rev. 2015)	
Items 1-8	Values/Comparative base	Item 9-15	Values
DCTTL	Several Arts., Constitution, Value=1	CSTINTLW	Yes; Art. 10, Value=1
CNTRY	The Republic of Colombia, Value=1	MDL	No refrences, Value=0
INTLW	Yes; Arts. 9 & 101, Value=1	ENDRNC	2015, No, Value=0
INTRGHT	General refrences, Value=1	SVRNGT	Several Arts. People, Value=1
INTTRT	Yes; several Arts., Value=1	FRNINVST	No refrences, Value=0
INTRTCNT	Inferior; Value=0	FRNTRD	Yes; several Arts., Value=1
INTORGS	Yes; several arts., Value=1	HDFRNAFRS	Yes; several Arts., Value=1
TOTALS	10 Values		

Fig. 3.6 General evaluation of the Colombia constitution based on international law

- CNTRY the constitution refers to the Republic as the type of country and government 184 times.
- INTLW, Arts. Nine and 109 refer to IL, defining Colombia's external relations based on national sovereignty and recognizing IL's principles approved by the state.
- INTRGHT Art. 93 provides incorporated international treaties and agreements by Congress that recognize HR and prohibit their limitation, put them superior to the national ones, and prioritize domestic ones even in states of emergency. The rights and duties mentioned in this constitution shall be interpreted by international treaties on HR incorporated by Colombia.
- INTTRT, Several Arts. Provide international treaties references; validation of treaties is finally through Congress approval. In case Congress did not approve the treaty, the application will suspend.
- INTRTCNT, Since the treaties have to be incorporated by presidential sign and congressional approval, the IL is considered inferior, and this item has no value.
- INTORGS, IOs has been referred to in several arts.
- CSTINTLW, however not directly, principles of IL are in use of interpretation which may allow to value it as positive.
- MDL, However, the constitution mentioned administration models; they are not related and pre-designed; therefore, the value is zero.

- ENDRNC, the constitution faced many amendments since its establishment in 1991; the one here referred to is 2015, which has no clue to vernacularization and valued zero.
- SVRNGT, the people of Colombia, is the owner and exercises the sovereign power, represented through constitutional institutions described in the constitution. Several articles refer to it and state that sovereignty resides exclusively in the people from whom public power emanates.
- FRNINVST, the constitution provides a National Investment Plan community that did not refer to foreign investment, and the item value is zero.
- FRNTRD, Several arts. e.g., one hundred eighty-nine defining the presidential powers and directly refer to foreign trade or art. That regulates foreign trade and specify the international exchange system and the Board of Directors of the Bank of the Republic in agreement with the functions which the constitution assigns, brought one value to this item.
- HDFRNAFRS, However, the constitution did not directly mention the head of foreign affairs; it provides an Advisory Committee on Foreign Relations as a president's consultative body.

So far, the Constitution of Colombia had the most rank compared to the Constitution of Azerbaijan, Finland, and South Africa; While it got ten values, the South African one got the least, 6 Finland 7 and Azerbaijan 8. The evaluation continues using the number of referred rights in the constitution.

3.2 Application of Rights Classification

Following section three of chapter four, rights classification, the same table and method will concern and create a rank of rights numbers in a constitution, here called the specific index of the rights, which contains 108 codes provided in six different tables as rights, indigenous rights, freedoms, equalities, protection, and other provisions. These tables may use in separately and later use their results together. The constitution's total result will show the number and type of the rights provided in the constitution and align, here HR treaties that the state of the examined constitution incorporated. Some of the rights will match the international one, and some do not, the one that matches, are the final result of the evaluation and provide the rank of the constitution compared to others. This result shows the international ranks and may be used in further analysis to see if it is potential for a revolution?

The total number of rights is 108; a category of 48 ones will be applied in one of the above sample constitutions, here, Azerbaijan. For the other parts, just the codes are sorted here.

Number and Kinds of Rights in the Constitution of Azerbaijan

Rights	Article	Value	Rights	Article	Value
INALRGHT	24	1	OMBDS	130	1
DGNT	24	1	PTNRGHT	57	1
LFE	27	1	ACDMCFRRGHT	No Refernces	0
CLTRRGHT	40	1	ARMSRGHT	No Refernces	0
SLFDTMNRGHT	No Refernces	0	NOMILRGHT	76 & 94	1
RMNRRGHT	No Refernces	0	DVLPRSNLTRGHT	No Refernces	0
HLTHCRRGHT	41	1	MRGRGHT	34	1
STANDLIV	12	1	FNDFAMRGHT	No Refernces	0
LISRRGHT	37	1	OCPTNRGHT	35	1
STRIKRGHT	36	1	FRMRKTRGHT	No Refernces	0
WRKRGHT	35	1	BSNSRGHT	59	1
APLJDCLDCSNRGHT	65	1	PROPRGHT	29	1
CNSLRGHT	61	1	TRNSFRPRPRGHT	No Refernces	0
EXMWTRGHT	63	1	TESTATERGHT	No Refernces	0
FRTRLRGHT	No Refernces	0	INFRGHT	No Refernces	0
PRTRLRGHT	127	1	OVRTHRRGHT	74, not granted, criminalized	0
PBTRLRGHT	127	1	PRVCRGHT	No Refernces	0
SPDTRLRGHT	No Refernces	0	LIBELRGHT	No Refernces	0
JRTRL	No Refernces	0	CTRNCRGHT	refrence not relevant	0
TRLLNG	127	1	CHLDRGHT	17	1
AMPRRGHT	No Refernces	0	SHLTRRGHT	No Refernces	0
JUDCRTS3	60	1	DBTRSRGHT	No Refernces	0
HRGHTCMSN	No Refernces	0	TOTALS	24 Values	

Fig. 3.7 Index of rights in the constitution of Azerbaijan

3.2.1 Azerbaijan Index of Constitutional Rights

Here a designed table containing data extracted from the Azerbaijan constitution based on the modern category subsection three of part four from chapter four is examined. The same tables of indexes containing the Indigenous Rights codes, Freedoms in the Constitution, Equalities, Protection, and Related Provisions in the Azerbaijan constitution may be applied, and the result will be used in the following procedure of the evaluation (Fig. 3.7).

3.2.2 Azerbaijan Values of Constitutional Rights

The figure provided the rights type and article reference in the Constitution of Azerbaijan. Here value is considered per each; therefore, the total number of values in this constitution is 24. In the next step, these values are examined in the incorporated HR treaties by Azerbaijan. After that, the result needs a crosscheck to provide the final evaluation result.

Azerbaijan CR values are below listed; their constitutional references are provided in the chart.

Value.1. INALRGHT
Value.2. DGNT
Value.3. LFE
Value.4. CLTRRGHT
Value.5. HLTHCRRGHT

Value.6. STANDLIV
Value.7. LISRRGHT
Value.8. STRIKRGHT
Value.9. WRKRGHT
Value.10. APLJDCLDCSNRGHT
Value.11. CNSLRGHT
Value.12. EXMWTRGHT
Value.13. PRTRLRGHT
Value.14. OMBDS
Value.15. PTNRGHT
Value.16. CHLDRGHT
Value.17. NOMILRGHT
Value.18. MRGRGHT
Value.19. OCPTNRGHT
Value.20. BSNSRGHT
Value.21. PROPRGHT
Value.22. PBTRLRGHT
Value.23. TRLLNG
Value.24. JUDCRTS3

3.3 Incorporated Human Rights Treaties

Almost any country in the international community has been a member of the UN charter and some of the international HR treaties; as a sample, since becoming a party to the UN charter, Azerbaijan has incorporated many HR treaties, and above examination of its constitution shows that it explicitly incorporated international treaties as an inalienable substantive part of the legal system. Azerbaijan joined many different HR treaties and their protocols, the basic ones discussed above are below; the complete list and declarations, if any, are available at the OHCHR indicator.[1]

3.3.1 Azerbaijan Incorporated Human Rights Treaties (Obligations)

(1) ICERD, accession in 1996
(2) ICCPR, accession in 1992
(3) ICCPR-OP1, accession in 2001
(4) ICCPR-OP2, accession in 1992
(5) CEDAW, accession in 1995

[1] United Nations Human Rights Office of the High Commissioner, "Ratification of 18 International Human Rights Treaties" (January 2019). http://indicators.ohchr.org.

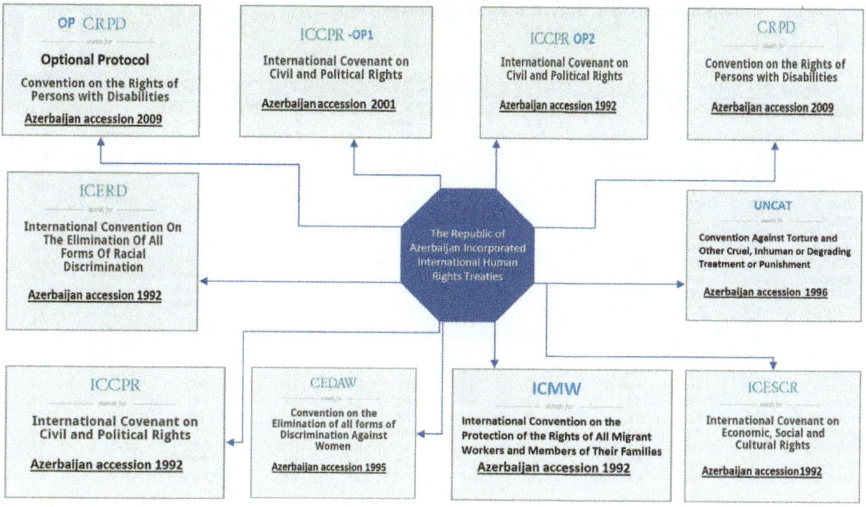

Fig. 3.8 Azerbaijan incorporated human rights treaties

(6) UNCAT, accession in 1996
(7) ICESCR, accession in 1992
(8) ICMW, accession in 1992
(9) CRPD, accession in 2009
(10) OP-CRPD, accession in 2009 (Fig. 3.8).

3.3.2 Azerbaijan Cross Checked Constitutional and Human Rights (Obligations)

Az Azerbaijan constitution considers international HR inalienable substantive part of the legal system and gained 24 values in the above application of HR classification. Now there is a need for a crosscheck of the extracted rights coded in the table with the ones provided in any of the above international HR treaties (Fig. 3.9).

These cross-checks and visuals not only show the weight of each international HR treaty in the Constitution of Azerbaijan but also shows standard-based for those constitutions which have the same obligation, whether like Azerbaijan, that considers incorporated IL obligations inalienable to the legal system or other constitutions consider IL inferior however they incorporate IL treaties. E.g., the Constitution of the Republic of Azerbaijan's weight of IL concerning ICERD is seven rights. To interpret the column of ICERD, it shows the rank of the Constitution of the Republic of Azerbaijan as five, i.e., the Constitution of Azerbaijan provides seven international HR obligations. DGNT, CLTRRGHT, HLTHCRRGHT, WRKRGHT, PTNRGHT, MRGRGHT, and PROPRGHT are the Constitution's HR values of Azerbaijan (Fig. 3.10).

Constitutional and Human Rights Crossed Check/International Human Rights Obligation

Rights	Constitutional Article	Preamble=P.	No References=N.R.		Several Articles=S.A.					
		ICERD	ICCPR	ICCPR-OP1	ICCPR-OP2	CEDAW	UNCAT	ICESCR	ICMW	CRPD	OP-CRPD
INALRGHT	24	N.R.	P.	N.R.	N.R.	Article 11	N.R.	P.	N.R.	P.	N.R.
DGNT	24	P.	P. & Article 10	N.R.	P.	P.	N.R.	P. & Article 13	Article 17	Several Refrences	N.R.
LFE	27	N.R.	Article 6	N.R.	P.	N.R.	N.R.	N.R.	Article 9	Artile 10	N.R.
CLTRRGHT	40	Article 5	P.	N.R.	N.R.	N.R.	N.R.	P. & Article 3	P.	Several Refrences	N.R.
HLTHCRRGHT	41	Article 5	N.R.	N.R.	N.R.	Article 11	N.R.	Article 12	N.R.	Article 25	N.R.
STANDLIV	12	N.R.	N.R.	N.R.	N.R.	N.R.	N.R.	Article 11	N.R.	Article 28	N.R.
LISRRGHT	37	N.R.	N.R.	N.R.	N.R.	N.R.	N.R.	Artile 7	N.R.	Article 30	N.R.
STRIKRGHT	36	N.R.	N.R.	N.R.	N.R.	N.R.	N.R.	Article 8	N.R.	N.R.	N.R.
WRKRGHT	35	Article 5	N.R.	N.R.	N.R.	Article 11	N.R.	Article 6	S.A	Article 27	N.R.
APLJDCLDCSNRGHT	65	N.R.	N.R.	N.R.	N.R.	N.R.	N.R.	N.R.	N.R.	N.R.	N.R.
CNSLRGHT	61	N.R.	Article 14	N.R.	N.R.	N.R.	Not Relevant	N.R.	Article 18	Not Relevant	N.R.
EXMWTRGHT	63	N.R.	Article 14	N.R.	Not Relevant	N.R.	N.R.	N.R.	Article 18	N.R.	N.R.
PRTRLRGHT	127	N.R.	Article 9	N.R.	N.R.	N.R.	N.R.	N.R.	Artic;e 16	N.R.	N.R.
OMBDS	130	N.R.	N.R.	N.R.	N.R.	N.R.	N.R.	N.R.	N.R.	N.R.	N.R.
PTNRGHT	57	Article 15	N.R.	Article 7	N.R.	N.R.	N.R.	N.R.	N.R.	N.R.	N.R.
CHLDRGHT	17	N.R.	N.R.	N.R.	N.R.	N.R.	N.R.	N.R.	N.R.	P. and Article 3	N.R.
NOMILRGHT	76 & 94	N.R.	N.R.	N.R.	N.R.	N.R.	N.R.	N.R.	N.R.	N.R.	N.R.
MRGRGHT	34	Article 5	Article 23	N.R.	N.R.	S.A.	N.R.	N.R.	N.R.	N.R.	N.R.
OCPTNRGHT	35	N.R.	N.R.	N.R.	N.R.	N.R.	N.R.	N.R.	N.R.	N.R.	N.R.
BSNSRGHT	59	N.R.	N.R.	N.R.	N.R.	N.R.	N.R.	N.R.	N.R.	Article 27	N.R.
PROPRGHT	29	Article 5	N.R.	N.R.	N.R.	N.R.	N.R.	N.R.	N.R.	Article 12	N.R.
PBTRLRGHT	127	N.R.	N.R.	N.R.	N.R.	N.R.	N.R.	N.R.	N.R.	N.R.	N.R.
TRLLNG	127	N.R.	Article 14	N.R.	N.R.	N.R.	N.R.	N.R.	Article 16	N.R.	N.R.
JUDCRTS3	60	N.R.	N.R.	N.R.	N.R.	N.R.	N.R.	N.R.	N.R.	N.R.	N.R.

Fig. 3.9 Azerbaijan cross checked constitutional and human rights

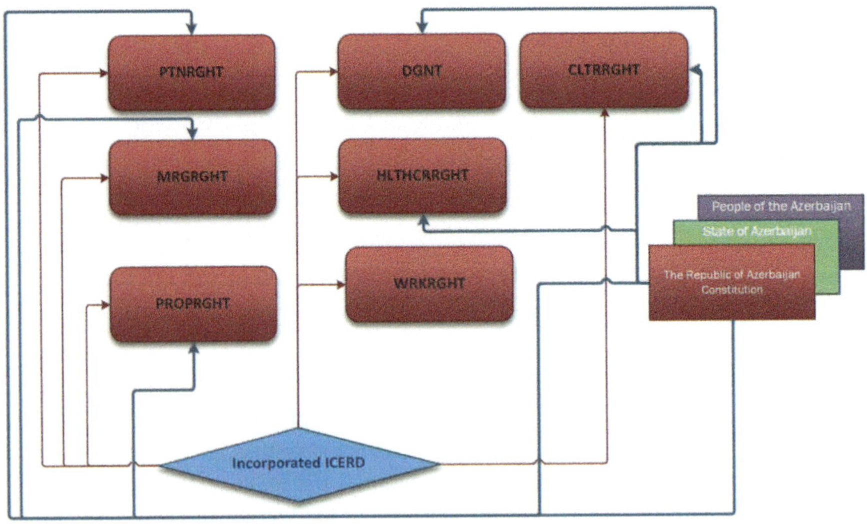

Fig. 3.10 Rank seven of the constitution of Azerbaijan

In the total of the incorporated HR treaties, each treaty has its values, and some values have a cross cover with the other ones like the below chart, which shows the raw evaluation. For a pure and separated result, there need addition and subtraction of cross-covered values (Figs. 3.11 and 3.12).

Every HR contains a core with the quality of a rule. When a case falls within the adequately defined scope of applying that rule, the rule determines the outcome without any further operation of balancing. Hence, the inviolability of the essential

ICERD	DGNT	CLTRRGHT	HLTHCRRGHT	WRKRGHT	PTNRGHT	MRGRGHT	PROPRGHT		
ICCPR	INALRGHT	DGNT	LFE	CLTRRGHT	CNSLRGHT	EXMWTRGHT	PRTRLRGHT	MRGRGHT	TRLLNG
ICCPR-OP1	PTNRGHT								
ICCPR-OP2	DGNT	LFE							
CEDAW	INALRGHT	DGNT	HLTHCRRGHT	WRKRGHT	MRGRGHT				
UNCAT									
ICESCR	INALRGHT	DGNT	CLTRRGHT	HLTHCRRGHT	STANDLIV	LISRRGHT	STRIKRGHT	WRKRGHT	
ICMW	DGNT	LFE	CLTRRGHT	CNSLRGHT	EXMWTRGHT	PRTRLRGHT	TRLLNG		
CRPD	INALRGHT	DGNT	CLTRRGHT	STANDLIV	LISRRGHT	WRKRGHT	CHLDRGHT	BSNSRGHT	PROPRGHT
OP-CRPD									

Fig. 3.11 Raw evaluation based on human rights treaties

ICERD	DGNT	CLTRRGHT	HLTHCRRGHT	WRKRGHT	PTNRGHT	MRGRGHT	PROPRGHT		
ICCPR	INALRGHT	DGNT	LFE	CLTRRGHT	CNSLRGHT	EXMWTRGHT	PRTRLRGHT	MRGRGHT	TRLLNG
ICCPR-OP1	PTNRGHT								
ICCPR-OP2	DGNT	LFE							
CEDAW	INALRGHT	DGNT	HLTHCRRGHT	WRKRGHT	MRGRGHT				
ICESCR	INALRGHT	DGNT	CLTRRGHT	HLTHCRRGHT	STANDLIV	LISRRGHT	STRIKRGHT	WRKRGHT	
ICMW	DGNT	LFE	CLTRRGHT	CNSLRGHT	EXMWTRGHT	PRTRLRGHT	TRLLNG		
CRPD	INALRGHT	DGNT	CLTRRGHT	STANDLIV	LISRRGHT	WRKRGHT	CHLDRGHT	BSNSRGHT	PROPRGHT

Fig. 3.12 Cross covered values

core of any HR is an essential step in the assessment of permissible limitations to the broader human right surrounding that core. Each HR approaches contain an essential or inviolable core, which needs to be emphasized that the notion of a core is just a metaphor. Some HR are complex umbrella concepts that host several quite different substantive elements or attributes. E.g., the Art. 17 of the ICCPR's provisions on the right to privacy lists family, home, correspondence, honor, and reputation, in addition to privacy itself, as compasses protected as HR. It is understandable that all or several interconnected, but separately identifiable, attributes of a complex HR may contain own core areas and therefore a single HR treaty provision multiple cores.[2]

3.4 Evaluation of the Constitution of Azerbaijan

In the complicated process above, each right of the constitution has been extracted, then the corresponding right in any international HR treaties which the state incorporated, found; In contrast, some CR has more provided in several incorporated treaties, the raw number of the values needed a calculation to reach the real number of the value. This chart provides a final evaluation of the Republic of Azerbaijan's Constitution based on its international HR obligations (Fig. 3.13).

---

[2] Shelton, *The Oxford Handbook of International Human Rights Law*. P536.

Fig. 3.13 Azerbaijan raw and final score of the constitution

DGNT	7 times
INALRGHT	4 times
PTNRGHT	2 times
LFE	3 times
WRKRGHT	4 times
CLTRRGHT	5 times
HLTHCRRGHT	3 times
CNSLRGHT	2 times
STANDLIV	2 times
EXMWTRGHT	2 times
PROPRGHT	2 times
MRGRGHT	3 times
LISRRGHT	2 times
PRTRLRGHT	2 times
STRIKRGHT	1 time
TRLLNG	2 times
CHLDRGHT	1 time
BSNSRGHT	1 time
Pure Value=8	Raw Value=48

Chapter 4
Transnational Evaluation of Constitutions

Abstract This study tries to produce a new ground for understanding the multidimensional concepts such as rights simultaneously for the people and humankind in international law and constitutional law with transnational connections. The impacts of transnational legal orders within nation-states are globalized in the modern international law and spectacles with normative and empirical-analytical lenses on constitutional and human rights while looking at international law and governance through constitutionalist glasses. International human rights law can have a significant impact on national systems, here constitutions. National constitutions may look at international and regional human rights norms to interpret and develop their national regulations. International and regional human rights norms can help national constitutional rights mechanisms in different ways, such as providing a base for the human rights claim on international or regional law. Such has been provided via the national constitution; or has contrarily been incorporated into national law. The use of the international and regional human rights law to interpret constitutional provisions and as a standard of protection increases ("Compilation of International Norms and Standards Relating to Disability."). Not only that but also the evolution of international law called fragmentation also directs and denotes both a process and its result. It first refers to the dynamic growth of new and specialized sub-fields of international law, secondly to the rise of new actors beside states, and thirdly to new types of international norms outside the acknowledged sources. It is smoothly started by ratifying human rights treaties and simultaneously constitutional amendments during the times and had a significant growth by the emergence of new states and constitutions after the breakdown of the communist bloc in 1989. The stable bi-polar world order shift to a host of multilateral treaties (Peters, "Constitutional Fragments—On the Interaction of Constitutionalization and Fragmentation in International Law." P3.). E.g., there is a five-part conceptual typology of the different ways that domestic courts can use foreign law: As (1) binding law, (2) a nonbinding norm, (3) an interpretive aid, (4) a basis for functional comparison, and (5) factual information (Jackson, Tolley, and Volcansek, *U*, Suny Series in the Foundations of the Democratic State. P48.). The comparative study of international law, human rights, and constitutional law have emerged as the new frontier of scholarship. Scholars and constitution drafters are increasingly using comparative methods in updating and upgrading conceptual and

A. Shirvani, *Transnational Evaluation of Constitutions*, SpringerBriefs in Law,
https://doi.org/10.1007/978-981-16-2976-1_4

contextual experiences in their works; meanwhile, decision-makers, academics, and the general public alike tend to think that several normative orders coexist.

4.1 Normative and Empirical Profundity of International Law

International standards relating to HR protection, good governance, or even democracy is frequently incorporated into national constitutions. Since the origins of such standards frequently lie in national constitutions and the norm-creating process of national and international legal systems, the integration of international standards into national constitutions is to some extent the reimport of a product that has been modified and which has become more or less universalized in global discourse.

E.g., HR was conceived as legal entitlements 200 years ago on the national level. That conception was transferred to the international level after the Second World War. Today, the idea of the legal protection of HR flows back into the constitutional orders of those states which have otherwise not satisfied HR standards. International actors use IL's norms as a point of reference from which to evaluate a national constitution. Pertinent examples are international prescriptions (hard and soft) on democracy, including free and regular elections. They are used by international institutions, including the UN, as guidelines for the reform of a constitution.

4.1.1 Constitutions and International Law Subjects

In classical doctrine, the classical international system's sole constituents were states, and they are IL subjects. States were born nominally equal and free and were endowed with imprescriptible rights (the so-called fundamental rights of states), purportedly enshrined in UNGA Resolution 2625 (XXV). Derogations from this natural state of freedom were only possible through consent, or perhaps through the actions of "great" states that dominated the system, despite the nominal rule of sovereign equality. The term state was used thirty-four times in the UN charter in many ways, such as for admission to the UN bringing a question concerning international peace and security before it; add to it for being a member of the International Court of Justice. However, the fundamental question about statehood concerning the PL goes through the constitution and the ability to establish one in force.[1]

Now, the modern state system of the twentieth century purported to embody the principle of popular sovereignty. Sovereignty was no longer held uniquely by the

[1] James Crawford, "The Creation of States in International Law, Issues of Statehood before United Nations Organs" (Feb. 2010, Oxford Scholarship Online: Oxford, 06 Mar. 2016 2007). http://www.oxfordscholarship.com. P1.

person of the prince or the abstraction of the state but instead was vested collectively in all the constituents of the country. The authority to govern, and to represent the governed internationally, was to be based on the will of the people of the state. However, this process of transmitting the will of the people and thus legitimizing public acts was generally deceptive, as the international legal rules crafted by governments continued to assert that any effective administration reflected, by definition, the will of the people. Hence, governments that could maintain themselves through whatever means were entitled to benefit from the rights attached to the state's concept by constitution and incorporation of international treaties.[2]

4.1.2 Impact of International Law on Constitutions

The IL became a legal reality in the national legal system and effectively lighted other dimensions of the entire legal picture. The engagement of constitutions with IL offers a line of transmutation of constitutionalism. Generative of norms empirical matter of transnational interactions (National and IL interactions national and international level) as a practical matter, the interactions between legal systems, under conditions of pluralism, may be generative of norms that gradually congeal as constitutional norms.[3] Diffusion, i.e., transnational connections (mentioned in the title) and influence on constitutional drafters, may appear in four possible processes: A. competition, B. Coercion, C. Learning, and D. Acculturation.

Uses and Scope of Comparative Constitutionalism the debate among scholars concerning the legitimate scope of the comparative method in CL centers around three defined positions.

(a) The first position maintains that both the problems of CL and their solution are, or ought to be, virtually the same across the spectrum of full-fledged constitutional democracies.
(b) The second position agrees that the problems of CL are the same for all but are convinced that the solutions to these problems are likely to differ from one constitutional polity to the next.
(c) The third position asserts that neither the constitutional problems nor their answers are likely to be the same for different constitutional democracies.

The first tends towards constitutional universalism and turns to comparative constitutionalism to elucidate the latter's proper standards and spotlight deviations.

The second is poised to highlight differences and place them in their proper context, thus shedding light on how different one constitutional system is from the next and why such constitutional systems—including the comparativists' own system—differ another.

---

[2]Armstrong, *Routledge Handbook of International Law*. P182–3.

[3]Sweet, "Constitutionalism, Legal Pluralism, and International Regimes." P633.

The third concludes that comparisons are most likely to be ultimately arbitrary and that the comparativists' choices and analyses are bound to be driven above all by ideology.

From the standpoint of the comparativists' own constitutional system, the first position offers a standard of identity that allows for the determination of conformity with the prescriptions of constitutionalism. The second position provides a measure of differentiation pointing to how and why one's constitution is distinct. The third position affords the means to refer selectively to apparent similarities and differences among constitutional jurisprudence to imprint a particular ideological gloss upon the comparativists' own.

Add to it, constitution-makers, academics, and the general public alike think that several normative orders coexist and are vying for allegiance and prominence; the general public alike tends to think that several normative orders coexist vying for allegiance and prominence.[4]

4.1.3 Applicable Transnational Definition

The difficulties of a comparative framework focusing on 'typologies' and 'differences across systems' of constitutional and IL are described in the views mentioned above. The significance reclines in the combination of transnational, constitutionalism, and IL, with each term taken to be hiding more than it is exposing. The term 'transnational' does not merely signify the extension of institutionalized or formalize normativity beyond borders, say, of nation-states or other jurisdictional confines. Instead, the term 'transnational' identifies intricate conjunction of spatial and conceptual dimensions: in labeling, on the one hand, the separation of rising and expanding spaces and, on the other, the construction of these places as artifacts for human activity, communication, and rationality, the term transnational is conceptual. To declare an activity transnational is not just the result of empirical observation, say, of a border-crossing.[5]

Philip Jessup first proposed using the term transnational law in the 1950s and serving as a focus of a new set of law problems that could not be fully subsumed within IL's field as then understood. However, to expand the breadth of the traditional boundaries and understanding of IL beyond that field's ability to contain it without becoming something else.[6]

---

[4] Jan Klabbers and Touko Piiparinen, *Normative Pluralism and International Law Exploring Global Governance*, ed. Elizabeth Andersen and Mortimer Sellers, ASIL Studies in International Legal Theory (United States of America: Cambridge University Press, 2013). P13.

[5] Rosenfeld and Sajó, *The Oxford Handbook of Comparative Constitutional Law*. P82.

[6] Larry Catá Backer's, "Principles of Transnational Law: The Foundations of an Emerging Field," *Law at the End of the Day*, 06 March 2007, http://lcbackerblog.blogspot.com/2007/03/principles-of-transnational-law.html.

4.1.4 Use of Ranking Methods

According to their substantial weight and significance, ranking the norms at stake should be assessed more subtly. Such a no formalist, substance-oriented perspective indicates that on the one side, specific less significant provisions in national constitutions would have to give way to relevant international norms. Inversely, fundamental rights guarantees should predominate over fewer mattering norms. This approach is already implicitly present in the emerging national constitutional practice of treating international HR treaties differently from ordinary IL, either by granting them precedence over state constitutions or using them, more than any other IL category, as guides for interpretation national constitutions.

It has to say; this approach does not offer stringent guidance because it is controversial which norms are more important in terms of substance and because it does not resolve clashes between CR on the one side and an international HR on the other. However, the key idea is that what counts is the substance, not the formal category of opposing norms. Such a flexible approach rises to correspond a better reaction with the state of globalization than does the meaning of a strict hierarchy, particularly in HR matters. From this perspective, IL and national constitutions find themselves in a fluid nature of interaction and reciprocal weight, based on discourse and mutual adaptation, but not in a hierarchical bond.

Previously, IL treated the effective government as the private entity entitled to exercise public authority within the state and represent it externally. The principle of periodic and genuine elections was not implemented with any seriousness. There is significant international opposition to the government's manifestly undemocratic practices, although it has to be admitted that the picture remains mixed. However, in several instances, the fundamental international constitutional principle that the authority to govern must be based on the will of the people being acted upon. These are cases where effectiveness and legitimacy are so far apart that representativeness's structural requirement must prevail over effectiveness. In this point, evaluating the legitimacy of constitutional agents' conduct applying competencies through public administrative acts, including governments, is no longer restricted to mechanical and circular validation through the effectiveness criterion.

In this regard, the abstract principle of legitimacy in the exercise of authority has already been translated into substantive fundamental dissociation rules. Accordingly, a sufficient authority can no longer claim to represent its constituents, either generally or about the state's specific functions; Bosnia, Burundi, Haiti, Iraq, Liberia, Rwanda, Somalia, Southern Rhodesia, South Africa, and so on. A sample of Constitution Rankings

(1) Length; it merely reports the total number of words measured by Microsoft Word in the constitution.

(2) Rights; There are a set of 117 different rights founds in an ongoing HR project in constitutions. The rights index indicates the number of these rights in any particular constitution.[7]

Now, it is sufficient merely to note several developments concerning the former the legitimacy of acts of governance at the national level. There is a growing recognition that the existence of the state itself must be based on an exercise of the will of the people. A significant constitutional change, such as dissolution, secession, or merger, occurs, a referendum, or at least an authentic decision by the democratically elected parliament, is required.

Similarly, for the generation of a new constitution, e.g., it will often now be endorsed through a referendum or a decision by a popular assembly due to an internal conflict. Moreover, in such circumstances, international peace support operations will invariably be involved in generating at least a first round of democratic elections to ensure that the new democratic consensus will indeed result in governance based on the will of the governed. This process is also in operation about entities such as the institutions of the EU. The referenda required in states which recently joined the EU, and which thus transferred significant public power to another layer of authority, can be used as an example in this respect as they can be said to reflect the acceptance of a legal rule requiring the validation of a significant transfer of competence from one layer to another through an act of choice by the relevant constituents.[8]

The critical need for evaluation means has increasingly come up in recent years. UN HR mechanisms are drawing a different picture and reporting on exclusion, the marginalization of communities, discrimination, the absence of participation, censorship, political repression or lack of an independent judiciary, and denial of economic and social rights. The HR movement is ubiquitous today. It has spread horizontally—across regions—and vertically—from the smallest unit in society to the loftiest international forum. International and national conflicts are often reported through an HR lens. There is virtually no issue without an HR dimension or angel, as well as CL. Searching the glittering pearls in the constellation of legal orders which democratic regimes operate needs special interdisciplinary instruments for extraction.

4.1.5 *Transnational Constitutionalism*

Transnational constitutionalism in a transparent definition is neither a normative order that emerges autonomously outside the nation-state's confines nor encompasses a distinct space of global governance without any relation to the community of states and the correlating measurements of law, namely national and international. Instead, transnational constitutionalism interprets the continuing evolution of constitutional

[7] "About the Comparative Constitution Project," accessed 1 Jan., 2016, http://comparativeconstitutionsproject.org/about-ccp/.

[8] Armstrong, *Routledge Handbook of International Law*. P186–7.

principles, instruments, and doctrines as an appropriate form of legal evolution on time. It radically disputes but does not oppose the distinction between the national and the international legal order. Scholars of public and private law in the 1950s suggested the conception of transnational law could aptly achieve the emergence of norm creation and implementation outside the confines of both private and public IL.[9] There are currently various transnational phenomena (including the NL that influences its borders) and an expanded IL array. IL is not a group of fragmented specialists and self-contained bodies of law, functioning in isolation from the others, but IL is a unified law system.[10]

4.1.6 Constitutions as the Roots of Human Rights

No doubt, general principles, and constitutions played as sources of HR law. The eighteenth-century HR declarations, which formed part of France and the United States' constitutions, were influential in the general approach taken to the underlying philosophy of the UDHR. The nature and content of the rights guaranteed were heavily inspired by the constitutional traditions of the fifty-five member states of the UN. It is arguable that given their relative novelty at the time of the UDHR negotiations, the economic and social rights the UDHR guaranteed may never have seen any light without reference to the constitutions of the Latin American and Communist states. The vast majority of HR instruments and provisions subsequently adopted at the national and international levels have built upon the guarantees elaborated in that timeless instrument.[11]

A significant legal evolution since World War II is the growing compliance of states to compel themselves constitutionally. Constitutions have been internationally standardized in what is called a "wave of constitutionalism." It led rights, HR, and CR to the forefront of these standards. Consequently, current constitutions have gradually expanded their list of rights. "First generation," "second generation," and "third-generation" in order, negative liberty rights have been complemented with positive socio-economic rights and then cultural and group rights. Currently, any typical constitution enumerates an extensive bill of rights that sets substantive constraints on democratic politics. The enforcement of these rights increasingly assigned in the controls of the judiciary. No less than eighty percent of the world's constitutions mandate the judiciary to overthrow democratic decisions that violate rights.[12]

---

[9]Rosenfeld and Sajó, *The Oxford Handbook of Comparative Constitutional Law*. P82.

[10]Peters, "Constitutional Fragments—On the Interaction of Constitutionalization and Fragmentation in International Law." P40.

[11]Shelton, *The Oxford Handbook of International Human Rights Law*. P221.

[12]Benedikt Goderis and Mila Versteeg, "The Transnational Origins of Constitutions" (6th Annual Conference for Empirical Legal Studies Paper (2011), Rational Choice and Constitutional Law Workshop Paper (2010), CentER Discussion Paper Series, 2013). P2.

Unique patterns are the Constitutional Court of Benin, which in various cases made reference to the ACHPR, and in some applied it directly; and the Supreme Court of Lesotho, which relied on the ACHPR together with other international HR treaties.[13]

4.1.7 Comparative Constitutionalism

Over the past decade, the discipline of comparative law has faced new tasks and challenges, arising mainly from the globalizing trends in contemporary life. It has been subjected to scrutiny from various perspectives when scholars began to ask hard questions about traditional approaches, such as the functional method. It has engaged in interdisciplinary discourse with history, sociology, IL, HR, and other fields. As a result, comparative law has become a vibrant and intellectually stimulating field of study and research, and it has advanced knowledge in a variety of areas and contexts.[14] Comparative constitutionalism, as a branch (particularly fragile one) of comparative law, has increasingly affected domestic CL because of a marked intensification of transnational crosscurrents. On the one hand, as constitutions are typically deeply embedded in national psyches and cultures, making comparisons seem hazardous. E.g., whereas it stands to reason that there be convergence on the subject of commercial contracts among industrialized democracies, unsurprisingly similarly phrased free speech provisions have resulted in widely diverging scopes of protection. On the other hand, despite these difficulties, there has been increasing use of comparative constitutional materials over the last couple of decades by both constitution-makers and constitutional adjudicators.[15]

4.2 Weighing International Law and Human Rights in Constitutional Laws

The result of this dissertation shows IL exercises a profound effect on the content of national constitutions. Although such an outcome may not become apparent at once, it is evident in modern constitutions or those recently amended. Some constitutional scholars and constitutional court judges, in particular, see this development with

[13]"Impact of the African Charter on domestic human rights in Africa," accessed 25 Mar., 2016, http://www.achpr.org/instruments/achpr/impact-on-domestic-human-rights/.

[14]Mathias Reimann and Reinhard Zimmermann, *The Oxford handbook of comparative law* (Oxford: Oxford University Press, 2007). Table of contents only http://www.loc.gov/catdir/toc/fy0706/2006497851.html.

Contributor biographical information http://www.loc.gov/catdir/enhancements/fy0723/2006497851-b.html.

Publisher description http://www.loc.gov/catdir/enhancements/fy0723/2006497851-d.html. P7.

[15]Rosenfeld and Sajó, *The Oxford Handbook of Comparative Constitutional Law*. P48.

skepticism. However, this development is unavoidable if one accepts that the national legal systems contribute significantly to maintaining peace and stability in the country concerned and the region. The effect of IL targets HR standards and institutional principles such as the separation of powers, the rule of law, or good governance. If one assesses the academic discussion as well as the discussion in HR institutions such as the HRC, it is mainly the application and implementation of HR that has given rise to controversy. Despite that, the common ground is much broader than many of the controversial discussions seem to suggest. This common ground appears to be a solid basis for further progressive developments.[16]

There are at least three statuses in part effective from the standpoint of the comparativists constitutional system.

The one offers a standard of identity for the determination of conformity with the prescriptions. The one provides a standard of distinctions leading to how a constitution is different. Moreover, the one affords the midpoints to refer selectively to apparent similarities and differences amid different constitutional jurisprudence to imprint a particular ideological gloss.[17]

The scope of the comparative analytical method among the constitutions concerns the enters around three defined positions.

(a) First, maintain that both the problems of CL and their solution are, or ought to be, substantially the same across the spectrum of full-fledged constitutional democracies.
(b) Second agrees that there are the same problems of CL in all of them. However, the solutions are likely to differ from one constitution to another.
(c) Third asserts that neither the constitutional problems nor their solutions are likely to be the same for different ones.

The first tends towards constitutional universalism and turns to comparative constitutionalism to elucidate the latter's proper standards and spotlight deviations. The second is poised to highlight differences and place them in their proper context, thus shedding light on how different constitutional systems are from another and why such constitutional systems differ. The last one concludes that comparisons are most likely to be sequentially optional and that the comparativists selections and analyses are bound to the above all by different doctrine.

Research outcomes may help ensure the dissemination and consolidation of a rights heritage between IL and CL, playing a unique role in conflict management. Evaluation of constitutions helps international analyze a constitution or draft constitution from by comparative and normative approach in a transnational perspective and provides below features:

- Offers a new approach and methods to the discussion of the relationship between CL and IL
- Draw multidimensional connections of IL and CL

[16]Grote and Röder, *Constitutionalism in Islamic Countries Between Upheaval and Continuity*. P88.
[17]Rosenfeld and Sajó, *The Oxford Handbook of Comparative Constitutional Law*. P50.

- Proposes a new understanding of CL discourse
- Provides comparative analyses of HR and CR in a geometric space
- Contributes to experimental constitutional issues in the light IL and HR
- Provides new categorization of constitutions
- Provides methods to identify international models of constitutions[18]
- Offers a new analysis of the stability of constitutions through HR weight of the constitutions
- Provides public and professional resource on comparative constitutional issues
- Provides a valuable overview with a critical assessment of constitution-making within movements of dynamic elements in PL
- Provides a base for investigating the efficacy of IL and HR on constitutions
- Advises an international-based legal framework for constitutions
- Provides a method of evaluation of constitutions
- Provides an IL characteristic recognition of the constitutions
- Provides methods of weighting HR in constitutions
- Provides a comparative analysis of HR treaties in constitutions.

Finally, this study may give rise to a long history of scholarly efforts seeking to analyze the patterns of successes and failures of constitutions, and this thesis falls within that tradition. There also ongoing progress to promote peace, justice, and HR development through constitutional matters, such as making process, interpretation, intranational literature. Moreover, voluntary acceptance of the guiding authority of IL over CL contributes to constitutional harmonization. Through these explorations, the thesis offers cross-disciplinary insights into the impact of recent political and economic changes on modern constitutionalism and an international evaluation method of the rule of law.

4.3 Computational Evaluation of Constitution

Computational methods are now on the run to facilitate the use of comparative analysis and indexation of constitutional texts plus conceptual grouping of their experimental results of the application, like endurance, chronicles of events, the number of amendments, referendums, elections, the balance of powers, construction of political parties, revolutions, decrees, pardon, etc. to design and render computational algorithms for digital democracy purposes and visualizations of the constitutional codes and their scope.

This essay is a step forward to digital democracy. It aims to demonstrate the ideas and interdisciplinary expertise of the constitutional and digital knowledge used in computational social science, particularly on text analysis of constitutions to develop digital constitutional patterns based on international and human rights.

[18]See Kristine Kalanges, *Religious Liberty in Western and Islamic Law Toward a World Legal Tradition* (New York: Oxford University Press, 2012).

This dissertation results may help projects that focus on formalizing constitutional texts and their experiments, developing automated reasoning procedures for compliance checking, and legal planning and regulatory analysis used in digital democracy.

By using legal informatics of constitutional texts in the automation and mechanization of legal analysis, current digital levels of legal efficiency, transparency, and access to legal systems worldwide become accessible.

The results and methodology used in this here might advance a general typology of the constitutional texts, e.g., republic, kingdom, democratic, Islamic, and so, and then study the chronicles, discourses and outsource resultants of specific groups for rendering a comparative analysis that provides data for the digital visualization of constitutional democracy. Such an outcome shall provide computational sources, including a mechanism of analysis, i.e., a software capable of text analysis of democratic semiotics that can be updated quickly.

Bibliography

1. The relationship between public international law and national law. https://sites.google.com/site/walidabdulrahim/home/my-studies-in-english/state-responsibility. Accessed 08 Mar 2016
2. Alston P, Crawford J (2000) The future of un human rights treaty monitoring. Cambridge University Press, Cambridge, New York. Sample text http://www.loc.gov/catdir/samples/cam032/99034665.html
3. Publisher description. http://www.loc.gov/catdir/description/cam0210/99034665.html
4. Table of contents. http://lcweb.loc.gov/catdir/toc/99034665.html
5. Armstrong D (2009) Routledge handbook of international law. In: Brunée J, Byers M, Jackson JH, Kennedy D (eds). Routledge, Oxon
6. Backer LC (2007) Principles of transnational law: the foundations of an emerging field. Law at the End of the Day, 06 Mar 2007. http://lcbackerblog.blogspot.com/2007/03/principles-of-transnational-law.html
7. Baehr PR (1999) Human rights: universality in practice. St. Martin's Press, New York, NY. Table of contents. http://lcweb.loc.gov/catdir/toc/98055203.html
8. Barsotti V, Carozza PG, Cartabia M, Simoncini A (2016) Italian constitutional justice in global context. Oxford University Press, Oxford, New York, NY
9. General principles relevant to international law. Icelandic Human Rights Center. http://www.humanrights.is/en/human-rights-education-project/human-rights-concepts-ideas-and-fora/part-i-the-concept-of-human-rights/general-principles-relevant-to-international-law. Accessed 25 Mar 2016
10. Commissioner, United Nations Human Rights Office of the High (2019) Ratification of 18 international human rights treaties, Jan 2019. http://indicators.ohchr.org
11. Compilation of international norms and standards relating to disability. United Nations. http://www.un.org/esa/socdev/enable/discom101.htm#15. Accessed 11 Mar 2016
12. Constitute. https://www.constituteproject.org/ontology/
13. Situation of human rights in the Syrian Arab Republic (2011) http://www.ohchr.org/EN/HRBodies/HRC/SpecialSessions/Session17/Pages/17thSpecialSession.aspx. Accessed 18 Mar 2014
14. Resolution Sc/10200 17 March 2011 (2011) https://www.un.org/press/en/2011/sc10200.doc.htm. Accessed 16 May 2016
15. Crawford J (2007) The creation of states in international law. In: Issues of statehood before United Nations organs, Feb 2010. Oxford Scholarship Online: Oxford, 06 Mar 2016. http://www.oxfordscholarship.com
16. d'Aspremont J (2011) Formalism and the sources of international law: a theory of the ascertainment of legal rules. In: Oxford monographs in international law. Oxford University Press, Great Britain
17. Definitions and classifications. Icelandic Human Rights Center. http://www.humanrights.is/en/human-rights-education-project/human-rights-concepts-ideas-and-fora/part-i-the-concept-of-human-rights/definitions-and-classifications. Accessed 10 Mar 2016

A. Shirvani, *Transnational Evaluation of Constitutions*, SpringerBriefs in Law,
https://doi.org/10.1007/978-981-16-2976-1

18. Dickson J, Gardner J (2001) Evaluation and legal theory. In: Legal theory today. Hart Pub., Oxford, Portland, OR
19. Another dimension to transnational constitutionalism? Outsider constitutional interpretation. http://www.iconnectblog.com/2012/11/article-review-vicki-jackson-and-rosalind-dixon-on-outsider-constitutional-interpretation/. Accessed 10 Oct 18
20. About the comparative constitution project. http://comparativeconstitutionsproject.org/about-ccp/. Accessed 1 Jan 2016
21. Elkins Z, Ginsburg T, Melton J (2016) Characteristics of national constitutions, version 2.0. http://comparativeconstitutionsproject.org/download-data/
22. The endurance of national constitutions (2009) Cambridge University Press. http://comparativeconstitutionsproject.org/chronology/. Accessed 24 Mar 2016
23. Research design (2016) Comparative constitutions project. http://comparativeconstitutionsproject.org/research-design-cataloging-the-contents-of-constitutions/. Accessed 22 Mar 2018
24. Gillroy JM (2013) An evolutionary paradigm for international law: philosophical method, David Hume, and the essence of sovereignty. In: Philosophy, public policy, and transnational law, 1st edn. Palgrave Macmillan, New York, NY. Cover image http://www.netread.com/jcusers2/bk1388/626/9781137376626/image/lgcover.9781137376626.jpg
25. Ginsburg T (2012) Comparative constitutional design. Cambridge University Press, New York
26. Ginsburg T, Dixon R (2011) Comparative constitutional law. In: Parisi F, Ginsburg T (eds) Research handbooks in comparative law. Edward Elgar Pub, UK and USA
27. Cataloging the contents of constitutions. Comparative constitutions project. http://comparativeconstitutionsproject.org/research-design-cataloging-the-contents-of-constitutions/. Accessed 27 Mar 2016
28. Constitution rankings. Comparative constitutions project. http://comparativeconstitutionsproject.org/ccp-rankings/. Accessed 26 Mar 2016
29. Goderis B, Versteeg M (2013) The transnational origins of constitutions. In: 6th annual conference for empirical legal studies paper (2011), rational choice and constitutional law workshop paper (2010), center discussion paper series
30. Goodhart ME (2016) Human rights: politics and practice, 3rd edn. Oxford University Press, Oxford, New York, NY
31. Grote R, Röder T (2012) Constitutionalism in Islamic countries between upheaval and continuity. Oxford University Press, New York
32. Hirschl R (2014) Comparative matters the renaissance of comparative constitutional law. Oxford University Press, New York
33. Hirschl R (2016) Early engagements with the constitutive laws of others: possible lessons from pre-modern religious law. Law Ethics Hum Rights 10(1):71–108. https://doi.org/10.1515/lehr-2016-0003
34. Hugues P, Versteeg M (2015) International law in national legal systems: an empirical investigation. Am J Int Law 109. Virginia public law and legal theory research paper No. 24, July 2015
35. Human rights indicators: a guide to measurement and implementation. The Office of the High Commissioner for Human Rights (OHCHR). http://www.ohchr.org/EN/Issues/Indicators/Pages/documents.aspx
36. Constitutional history of Tunisia. International IDEA. http://www.constitutionnet.org/country/constitutional-history-tunisia. Accessed 15 Jan 2017
37. Index (2016) The economist intelligence unit's democracy. The economist democracy index. The Economist, London. https://infographics.economist.com/2017/DemocracyIndex/
38. International norms and standards relating to disability. United Nations. http://www.un.org/esa/socdev/enable/comp001.htm. Accessed 11 Mar 2016
39. Jackson DW, Tolley MC, Volcansek ML (2010) Globalizing justice critical perspectives on transnational law and the cross. Volume Suny series in the foundations of the democratic state. State University of New York Press, Albany
40. Joerges C, Sand I-J, Teubner G (2004) Transnational governance and constitutionalism. In: International studies in the theory of private law. Hart Publishing, US and Canada

41. Joerges C, Petersmann E-U (2006) Constitutionalism, multilevel trade governance and social regulation. In: Studies in international trade law. Hart Publishing, North America (US and Canada)
42. Kalanges K (2012) Religious liberty in western and Islamic law toward a world legal tradition. Oxford University Press, New York
43. Klabbers J, Piiparinen T (2013) Normative pluralism and international law exploring global governance. In: Andersen E, Sellers M (eds) ASIL studies in international legal theory. Cambridge University Press, United States of America
44. Koskenniemi M. Methodology of international law. In: Max Planck encyclopedia of public international law [MPEPIL]
45. Oxford Public International Law, 11 Dec 2014 (2007) http://opil.ouplaw.com/view/10.1093/law:epil/9780199231690/law-9780199231690-e1440#
46. Preambles of constitutions—a comparative study of 194 current constitutions (2015) Constitution—making and constitutional change. http://constitutional-change.com/preambles-of-constitutions-a-comparative-study-of-194-current-constitutions/. Accessed 27 Mar 2016
47. Lynch M (2014) The Arab uprisings explained: new contentious politics in the Middle East. Columbia studies in Middle East politics. Columbia University Press, New York
48. Macklem P (2015) The sovereignty of human rights. Oxford University Press, Oxford, New York
49. Marciano A, Holcombe RG (2011) Constitutional mythologies: new perspectives on controlling the state. Studies in public choice. Springer, New York. Table of contents only. http://www.loc.gov/catdir/toc/fy12pdf01/2011934053.html
50. Melton J, Elkins Z, Ginsburg T (2013) Whither Scotland? An evaluation of a proposed constitutional plan. Towards a written Scottish constitution, Paris
51. Member states of the United Nations. United Nations. http://www.un.org/en/members/. Accessed 26 Mar 2016
52. Merry SE (2005) Human rights and gender violence translating international law into local justice. Chicago series in law and society. The University of Chicago Press, Chicago
53. Moellers C (2013) The three branches a comparative model of separation of powers. In: Loughlin M, McCormick JP, Walke N (eds) Oxford constitutional theory. Oxford University Press, Great Britain
54. Mubangizi JC (2004) Towards a new approach to the classification of human rights with specific reference to the African context. Afr Hum Rights Law J 4(1):14. http://www.ahrlj.up.ac.za/mubangizi-j-c#_ftnref5
55. Mutua MW (2007) Standard setting in human rights critique and prognosis. Human Rights Q 29:83. Buffalo legal studies research paper no. 2007–013. http://ssrn.com/abstract=1010947
56. Gender equality. https://www.un.org/en/sections/issues-depth/gender-equality/. Accessed 18 Mar 2018
57. O'Donoghue A (2014) Constitutionalism in global constitutionalisation. Cambridge University Press, United Kingdom
58. Report of the Ohchr mission to Egypt 27 March–4 April 2011 (2011) http://www.ohchr.org/Documents/Countries/EG/OHCHR_MissiontoEgypt27March_4April.pdf. Accessed 13 Nov 2013
59. Constitutional fragments—on the interaction of constitutionalization and fragmentation in international law (2015) Working paper. Centre for Global Constitutionalism, University of St. Andrews. http://papers.ssrn.com/sol3/papers.cfm?abstract_id=2591370. Accessed 26 Mar 2016
60. Global constitutionalism. http://www.mpil.de/en/pub/research/areas/public-international-law/global-constitutionalism.cfm. Accessed 06 Mar 2016
61. Peters A (2009) The merits of global constitutionalism. Indiana J Glob Leg Stud 16(2)
62. Peters A (2009) Supremacy lost: international law meets domestic constitutional law. Vienna Online J Int Const Law 3:28
63. Project, World Justice (2012–13) Rule of law index. Washington, DC. https://worldjusticeproject.org/our-work/publications/rule-law-index-reports/wjp-rule-law-index-2012-2013-report

64. The protocol and liaison service. United Nations. https://protocol.un.org/dgacm/pls/site.nsf/HSHGNFA.xsp. Accessed 18 Oct 2017
65. Lima Group countries say won't recognize new Maduro mandate, 05 Jan 2019. https://www.rappler.com/world/regions/latin-america/220338-lima-group-non-recognition-maduro. Accessed 07 Jan 2019
66. Reimann M, Zimmermann R (2007) The Oxford handbook of comparative law. Oxford University Press, Oxford. Table of contents only. http://www.loc.gov/catdir/toc/fy0706/2006497851.html
67. Contributor biographical information. http://www.loc.gov/catdir/enhancements/fy0723/2006497851-b.html
68. Publisher description. http://www.loc.gov/catdir/enhancements/fy0723/2006497851-d.html
69. Chronology of events (2011) Updated 2 Feb 2017. http://www.securitycouncilreport.org/chronology/syria.php?page=6. Accessed 18 Jan 2017
70. Un documents for Syria. http://www.securitycouncilreport.org/un-documents/syria/. Accessed 8 Apr 2016
71. Impact of the African charter on domestic human rights in Africa. http://www.achpr.org/instruments/achpr/impact-on-domestic-human-rights/. Accessed 25 Mar 2016
72. Classification of rights (1996) Constitution Society. http://www.constitution.org/col/class_right.htm. Accessed 13 Mar 2016
73. Rosenfeld M, Sajó A (2012) The Oxford handbook of comparative constitutional law. Oxford University Press, Great Britain. https://doi.org/10.1093/oxfordhb/9780199578610.013.0003
74. Ruppel OC, Scherr KM, Berndt AD (eds) Assessing progress in the implementation of Zimbabwe's new constitution
75. National, regional and global perspectives (2017) Recht Und Verfassung in Afrika—law and constitution in Africa. NOMOS, Deutschland. https://doi.org/10.5771/9783845283746-84
76. Comparative public law methodology in international investment law (2014) Eur J Int Law. https://www.ejiltalk.org/comparative-public-law-methodology-in-international-investment-law/. Accessed 17 Oct 2015
77. Secretary-general deplores killing of Yemeni protesters by security forces (2011) Updated 18 Mar 2011. http://www.un.org/apps/news/story.asp?NewsID=37811. Accessed 18 Nov 2013
78. Şen İG (2015) Sovereignty referendums in international and constitutional law. Springer International Publishing. https://doi.org/10.1007/978-3-319-11647-1
79. In quotes: reaction to Tunisian crisis (2011) BBC News Services. http://www.bbc.com/news/world-africa-12197681. Accessed 18 Nov 2013
80. Shaw MN (2008) International law. Cambridge University Press, United States of America
81. Shelton D (2013) The Oxford handbook of international human rights law. Oxford University Press, New York
82. Spotlights on health and rights history and categories of human rights. The Heilbrunn Department of Population and Family Health, Columbia University. http://healthandrights.ccnmtl.columbia.edu/human_rights/history_categories_human_rights.html. Accessed 10 Mar 2016
83. Sweet AS (2009) Constitutionalism, legal pluralism, and international regimes. Indiana J Glob Leg Stud 16(2):24
84. Tamanaha BZ (2011) The rule of law and legal pluralism in development. Hague J Rule Law 3(1):17. https://doi.org/10.1017/S1876404511100019
85. Trachtman JP (2013) The future of international law: global government. Asil studies in international legal theory. Cambridge University Press, United States of America
86. Tushnet MV, Fleiner-Gerster T, Saunders C (2013) Routledge handbook of constitutional law. Routledge handbooks. Routledge, Abingdon, Oxon, New York, NY. Table of contents only. http://www.loc.gov/catdir/toc/fy14pdf01/2012027701.html
87. Un official voices alarm at Egypt violence, cites 'major' problems with draft constitution (2012) http://www.un.org/apps/news/story.asp?NewsID=43706. Accessed 7 Jan 2013
88. Putting fundamental rights of persons with disabilities on the map, 2 Dec 2016. University of California. https://medicalxpress.com/news/2016-12-fundamental-rights-persons-disabilities.html. Accessed 16 Feb 2017

89. Versteeg M (2013) Law versus norms the impact of human rights treaties on constitutional rights. Virginia public law and legal theory research
90. Wellman C (2016) Constitutional rights—what they are and what they ought to be. Springer Berlin Heidelberg, New York, NY. Publisher description. https://www.loc.gov/catdir/enhancements/fy1615/2016937981-d.html
91. Table of contents only. https://www.loc.gov/catdir/enhancements/fy1615/2016937981-t.html
92. Young KG (2012) Constituting economic and social rights. In: Loughlin M, McCormick JP, Walker N (eds) Oxford constitutional theory. Oxford University Press, Great Britain

The manufacturer's authorised representative in the EU is Springer Nature Customer Service Centre GmbH, Europaplatz 3, 69115 Heidelberg, Germany. If you have any concerns regarding our products, please contact ProductSafety@springernature.com

Printed and bound by CPI Group (UK) Ltd, Croydon, CR0 4YY
01/10/2026
02226300-0003